OUTSMART SCIENCE

for ages 10 & up

MARK SHULMAN

KAPLAN

PUBLISHING

New York

This publication is designed to provide accurate and authoritative information in regard to the subject matter covered. It is sold with the understanding that the publisher is not engaged in rendering legal, accounting, or other professional service. If legal advice or other expert assistance is required, the services of a competent professional should be sought.

Vice President and Publisher: Maureen McMahon
Editorial Director: Jennifer Farthing
Development Editor: Kate Lopaze
Production Editor: Fred Urfer
Illustrations: Aaron Meshon
Photography: Veer, Inc
Typesetting: Marsha Swan
Interior design: Carly Schnur

Published by Kaplan Publishing, a division of Kaplan, Inc.
1 Liberty Plaza, 24th Floor
New York, NY 10006

Printed in the United States of America

May 2008
10 9 8 7 6 5 4 3 2 1

ISBN-13: 978-1-4195-5060-7

Kaplan Publishing books are available at special quantity discounts to use for sales promotions, employee premiums, or educational purposes. Please email our Special Sales Department to order or for more information at kaplanpublishing@kaplan.com, or write to Kaplan Publishing, 1 Liberty Plaza, 24th Floor, New York, NY 10006.

WHAT'S OUTSMART SCIENCE ALL ABOUT?

Congratulations! You're the proud owner (or reader) of the very finest *Outsmart Science* book you've ever seen. We know you're itching to open it up and take it for a spin...but first, please read this totally complicated introduction. We're sure you have a lot of questions about the book before you read all the questions *in* the book. Here are some questions we hope you'll ask.

WILL this book answer all of my questions?
That depends on what all your questions are. But it will answer all our questions—250 of them, if you're counting. And if our answers happen to match your questions, then the answer is a resounding YES!

HOW, exactly, do I use my new Outsmart book?
First of all, there are two questions on a page. But that's not all. Turn the page, and presto—you'll find two answers. That's twice the value! When you get to the end of a section, there are two bonus questions (we call them "bonus questions") for an extra challenge. When you finally get to the end of each section, take

iii

a victory lap around the building. Exercise is good for refreshing brain cells. Then you can move on to the next set of questions.

WHO is Mark Shulman, and WHAT makes him an authority on this topic?

Mark Shulman is the author of dozens (12s) of books for people just like you. His books have titles like *The Brainiac Box: 600 Facts Every Smart Person Should Know* AND *Attack of the Killer Video Book* AND *Mom and Dad Are Palindromes* AND *Secret Hiding Places (for Clever Kids)*. He took science in middle school and can still pass it today!

QUESTION 1

WHAT is an element?

ANSWER > > > >

• • • • • • • • •

QUESTION 2

WHAT is an atom?

ANSWER > > > >

OUTSMART SCIENCE

ANSWER 1

An element is a substance in its pure form. You can't break it down into another compound that has different properties, and neither can anyone else. It's also true that an element consists of atoms of one element.

• • • • • • • • •

ANSWER 2

An atom (a word that comes from the Greek, meaning "can't be divided") is (1) really, really small; (2) found in all common matter; (3) the smallest part of an element to keep all its chemical properties; and (4) actually can be divided.

QUESTION 3

WHAT are the three subatomic part(icle)s that an atom can be divided into?

ANSWER > > > >

• • • • • • • • •

QUESTION 4

WHAT is a molecule?

ANSWER > > > >

ANSWER 3

An atom can be divided into its electrons, protons, and neutrons.

• • • • • • • • •

ANSWER 4

When two atoms (or more) are joined together (chemically), a molecule is formed.
O_2 (oxygen) is a molecule, but it isn't a compound. But what is a compound, you ask? So do we. Flip to the next page...

CHEMISTRY

QUESTION 5

WHAT is a compound?

ANSWER > > > >

• • • • • • • • •

QUESTION 6

WHICH subatomic particles have a positive charge, and which have a negative charge?

ANSWER > > > >

OUTSMART SCIENCE

A compound is a molecule whose atoms contain at least two different elements. Dihydrogen oxide (H_2O) is a compound of hydrogen and oxygen, and carbon dioxide (CO_2) is a compound of carbon and oxygen. Remember, all molecules are compounds, but all compounds are not molecules.

• • • • • • • • •

Protons have a positive charge, and electrons have a negative charge. Neutrons are neutral and have no charge at all.

QUESTION 7

WHAT are the three states of matter?
(Think water.)

ANSWER >>>>

• • • • • • • • •

QUESTION 8

WHAT is known as the fourth state
of matter?

ANSWER >>>>

OUTSMART SCIENCE

ANSWER 7

Solid, liquid, and gas.

• • • • • • • • •

ANSWER 8

It isn't gas, liquid, or solid. It's plasma! It conducts electricity and, recently, TV shows.

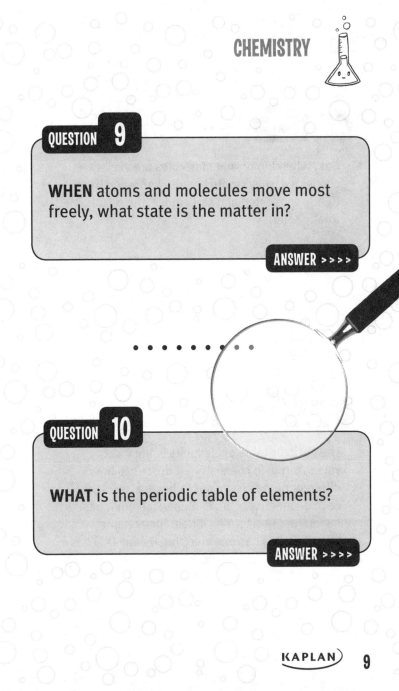

QUESTION 9

WHEN atoms and molecules move most freely, what state is the matter in?

ANSWER >>>>

QUESTION 10

WHAT is the periodic table of elements?

ANSWER >>>>

ANSWER 9

Gas. When atoms and molecules are loosely connected, they create liquids. And when they are tightly connected and can't move, the results are totally solid.

• • • • • • • • •

ANSWER 10

The periodic table of elements is the most valuable tool in chemistry—it describes the different properties of each chemical element. Each element appears in numerical order, based on how many electrons it has. For example, hydrogen (#1) has one electron. Helium (#2) has two electrons, and so on.

QUESTION 11

HOW many elements have been discovered (so far)?

ANSWER > > > >

• • • • • • • • •

QUESTION 12

WHAT super man's name is found on the periodic table of the elements?

ANSWER > > > >

ANSWER 11

There are currently 103 elements, and all of them are featured on the periodic table. Some elements, like hydrogen, oxygen, and carbon, are found in every living organism. Others, like lawrencium (under the table at #103), have a half-life of a few seconds and then decay beyond recognition, which is what usually happens under the table.

• • • • • • • •

ANSWER 12

ClArK is his name. Chlorine, argon, and potassium (atomic numbers 17, 18, 19) are his secret ingredients. You may wonder why potassium is represented with a K, and so do we.

CHEMISTRY

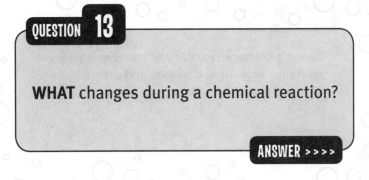

QUESTION 13

WHAT changes during a chemical reaction?

ANSWER > > > >

• • • • • • • • • •

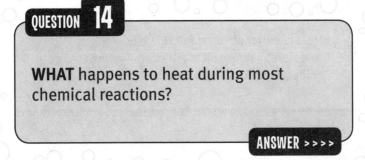

QUESTION 14

WHAT happens to heat during most chemical reactions?

ANSWER > > > >

ANSWER 13

During a chemical reaction the atoms in matter are rearranged into new, different, and occasionally life-threatening combinations of molecules.

• • • • • • • •

ANSWER 14

Heat is either absorbed or released. And, therefore, your result is either something that got colder (absorbed heat) or hotter (released heat).

QUESTION **15**

WHAT happens to the number of atoms in matter during a chemical reaction?

ANSWER > > > >

· · · · · · · · · ·

QUESTION **16**

WHAT does pH measure?

ANSWER > > > >

ANSWER 15

Trick question: Nothing happens. The number of
atoms (the matter's mass) stays the same even
after a chemical reaction.

• • • • • • • • •

ANSWER 16

pH measures the acidity (acid) or alkalinity (base)
of water or a solution. Acidity is the presence of
acid in the solution. Base is the lack of acid but the
presence of alkaline. Neutral is neutral.

QUESTION 17

WHICH color will litmus paper change to when dipped in an acid solution?

ANSWER >>>>

• • • • • • • • •

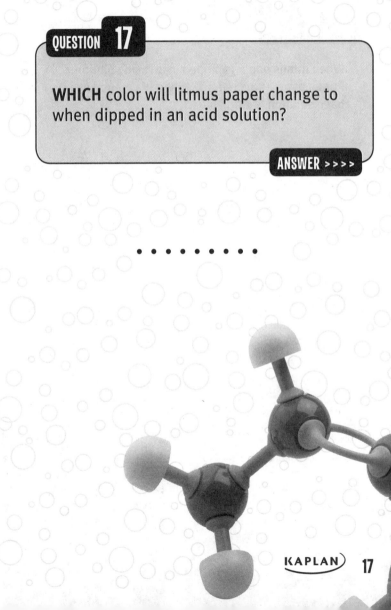

ANSWER **17**

When litmus paper is dipped in an acid solution, litmus paper turns red. FYI, when it's dipped in a base solution, it turns blue.

• • • • • • • •

QUESTION 18

HOW does matter change between solid, liquid, and gas?

ANSWER > > > >

• • • • • • • • •

QUESTION 19

WHICH two ways can matter change form without a chemical reaction?

ANSWER > > > >

ANSWER 18

The scientific answer: The molecular motion changes, usually due to heat. The unscientific answer: boiling and freezing.

• • • • • • • • •

ANSWER 19

Matter can freeze and matter can boil, and both without a chemical reaction.

QUESTION **20**

WHO studies rocks and the planet?

ANSWER > > > >

• • • • • • • • •

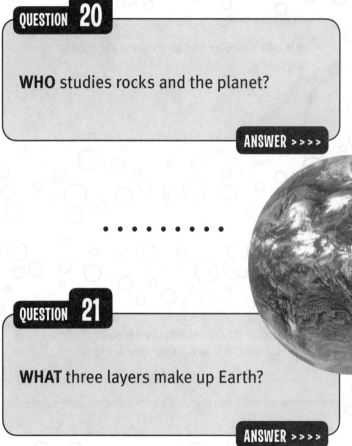

QUESTION **21**

WHAT three layers make up Earth?

ANSWER > > > >

ANSWER 20

Lots of people do. But geologists get paid for it, usually.

ANSWER 21

The core, the mantle, and the crust (or lithosphere). You live on the upper crust.

QUESTION 22

WHAT is the Earth's crust? **WHAT** is it made of?

ANSWER > > > >

• • • • • • • • •

QUESTION 23

WHERE on Earth is the planet's mantle?

ANSWER > > > >

The crust (also called the lithosphere) is the outermost surface of Earth. The top layer is soil (or dirt), and different rock layers come next, before reaching the mantle about 18 miles under your house.

• • • • • • • • •

The crust is Earth's outermost layer. The 1,800 miles beneath it is called the mantle, reaching all the way to the Earth's inner core. Imagine a grape-sized, candy-coated, chocolate treat with a peanut in the center. The candy coating is the crust. The chocolate is the mantle. The peanut is the core. Yum!

QUESTION 24

WHAT is the parent material of soil?

ANSWER > > > >

• • • • • • • • •

QUESTION 25

WHICH three chemicals are almost always found in the parent material of soil?

ANSWER > > > >

ANSWER 24

Parent material is what's in the bedrock below the soil. Minerals from the bedrock are the parent material, and they influence the soil, just like a sloppy mess influences the sponge you clean it with.

• • • • • • • •

ANSWER 25

In alphabetical order, calcium, nitrogen, and sulfur.

QUESTION 26

WHAT is plate tectonics?

ANSWER > > > >

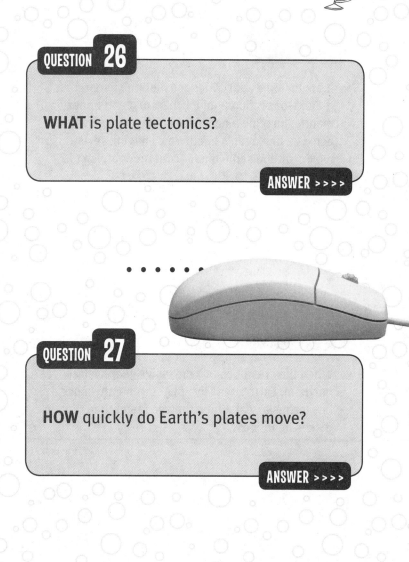

QUESTION 27

HOW quickly do Earth's plates move?

ANSWER > > > >

ANSWER 26

Plate tectonics describes the motion of enormous plates—or sections—of Earth's crust and upper mantle. Imagine a hairpiece sliding very slowly across a bald man's head. Now imagine several moving at the same time. Awful thought, isn't it?

• • • • • • • • •

ANSWER 27

When they're not causing massive geophysical mayhem, Earth's massive plates generally move a few inches a year. When they go faster than that, it makes headlines.

QUESTION **28**

WHY do Earth's plates shift?

ANSWER > > > >

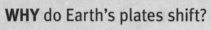

QUESTION **29**

WHEN the plates shift, what happens?

ANSWER > > > >

ANSWER 28

Earth's mantle is a restless place. It's extremely hot, but not consistent. As it gets (relatively) cooler and then heats back up (a process called convection), the mantle's molten contents expand and contract in very slow motion, causing plates to shift.

• • • • • • • • •

ANSWER 29

Earthquakes happen. Tsunamis happen, as a result of underwater earthquakes. Mountains happen as landforms are redefined. And volcanoes happen as bubbling hot magma flows through new openings in Earth's surface.

QUESTION 30

WHAT do earthquakes and fingernail biting have in common?

ANSWER >>>>

• • • • • • • • •

QUESTION 31

WHAT are stalagmites and stalactites?

ANSWER >>>>

ANSWER 30

Stress! In the case of earthquakes, stress exists at the planet's faults, where the tectonic plates are either colliding or separating. In the case of fingernails, relax! Problems have a way of working themselves out.

• • • • • • • • •

ANSWER 31

These icicle-shaped formations are usually found in caves. They're made from a mix of dripping water, calcium, and other minerals. Stalactites hang from the ceiling and drip down, forming stalagmites that rise up from the ground. (Remember, c is for ceiling and g is for ground.)

QUESTION **32**

WHAT is sedimentary rock?

ANSWER > > > >

• • • • • • • • • •

QUESTION **33**

WHAT is metamorphic rock?

ANSWER > > > >

ANSWER **32**

Sedimentary rock (meaning settled rock) is formed from sand, dust, seashells, and sea creatures that settled at the ocean's bottom many millions of years ago. Over time, the layers hardened into rock. Limestone is a sedimentary rock popular with fossil hunters.

• • • • • • • • •

ANSWER **33**

Metamorphic rock (meaning changed rock) lies beneath sedimentary rock. Heat and pressure inside of Earth cause limestone, for example, to morph into marble over a very long time. Shale also turns into slate this way.

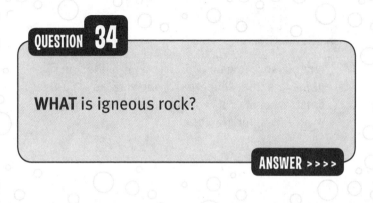

QUESTION **34**

WHAT is igneous rock?

ANSWER >>>>

. . . .

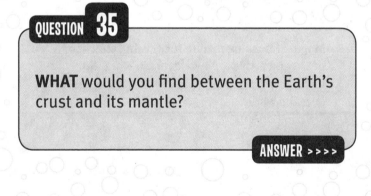

QUESTION **35**

WHAT would you find between the Earth's crust and its mantle?

ANSWER >>>>

Igneous rock (meaning fired rock) is melted rock, or magma, that squeezes through cracks in Earth's crust. When it cools and hardens, it's one tough rock. Take it for granite.

· · · · · · · · ·

Magma (meaning melted rock) is the checkpoint between Earth's top two layers. It's hot. It's bubbly. And it's the inspiration for volcanoes all over the world.

QUESTION 36

WHAT is the Earth's mantle made of?

ANSWER > > > >

• • • • • • • • •

QUESTION 37

WHAT is the Earth's core made of?

ANSWER > > > >

ANSWER 36

Solid rock. Hot rock. 1,000°–3,000° rock. And it rocks from about 18 miles underfoot to about 1,800 miles.

• • • • • • • • •

ANSWER 37

Heavy metal. Around 80 percent is iron—the rest is thought to be liquid iron, nickel, and other metals. The inner core may even be a single iron crystal. You can proudly say you live on the densest planet in the solar system.

QUESTION 38

HOW big is Earth's core?

ANSWER > > > >

• • • • • • • • •

QUESTION 39

HOW long is the radius of Earth?

ANSWER > > > >

ANSWER 38

The core is divided into two parts: the inner core and the outer core. The radius of the outer core is about 2,200 miles. The radius of the central inner core is about 800 miles.

• • • • • • • • •

ANSWER 39

All in all, Earth's radius is about 4,000 miles from surface to core. If you're going, you won't need a sweater. It'll be warm when you get there.

QUESTION **40**

WHAT on Earth is the geosphere?

ANSWER >>>>

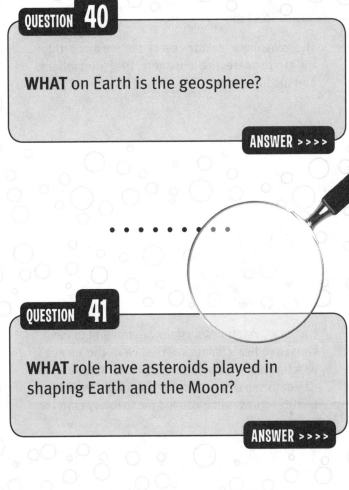

QUESTION **41**

WHAT role have asteroids played in shaping Earth and the Moon?

ANSWER >>>>

ANSWER **40**

The geosphere includes every system on Earth: the atmosphere, the biosphere, the hydrosphere, and the lithosphere.

• • • • • • • • •

ANSWER **41**

On Earth, asteroid collisions are thought to have caused radical climate shifts such as the ice ages, which wiped out dinosaurs and other species. It's easier to see what asteroids did for the Moon's beauty—guess what caused those lovely craters?

QUESTION 42

WHAT is a rock cycle, and did cave dwellers ride them?

ANSWER >>>>

QUESTION 43

WHICH word describes the speed of Earth's usual geologic processes (in the cases that do not involve asteroid collisions)?

ANSWER >>>>

ANSWER 42

A rock cycle is a series of changes that rocks can go through. Under different conditions, igneous, sedimentary, or metamorphic rock can change into other kinds of rock. If cave dwellers did ride them, it was downhill all the way.

• • • • • • • •

ANSWER 43

Slow. Or perhaps, glacial. Generally, real change takes place over very long periods of time. Like epochs or eras. We're talking millions of years.

QUESTION **44**

WHAT exactly do volcanoes change on Earth?

ANSWER > > > >

• • • • • • • • •

QUESTION **45**

WHAT comes out of a volcano when it erupts?

ANSWER > > > >

ANSWER 44

Those murderous, molten mountains change the very topographic surface of the Earth. When the bubbling, red-hot magma cools down, mountains are raised, islands are formed, seashores are altered, and mapmakers everywhere get back to work.

• • • • • • • •

ANSWER 45

Mostly there's magma (molten rock) from inside Earth's surface. Once it comes out, it's called lava. Volcanic ash and rocks and dust also emerge, as would skeletons and buried treasure if they happened to be near the source of the eruption at the time and didn't melt easily.

QUESTION 46

WHAT are fossils?

ANSWER > > > >

• • • • • • • •

QUESTION 47

HOW do innocent little animals and plants get turned into fossils?

ANSWER > > > >

ANSWER 46

Fossils are the remains of animals, plants, eggs, or footprints...all turned into rocks or minerals.

• • • • • • • • • •

ANSWER 47

Since living things tend to decompose after they've bitten the dust, becoming a fossil isn't easy. The corpse in question has to be covered with sediment relatively soon, settle underwater, or become petrified. Natural decomposition is slowed or stopped. More sediment settles, hardens, and gradually becomes a rock cast of the original model. This can happen with footprints and other marks, too.

QUESTION 48

HOW old are the oldest fossils?

ANSWER > > > >

. . . .

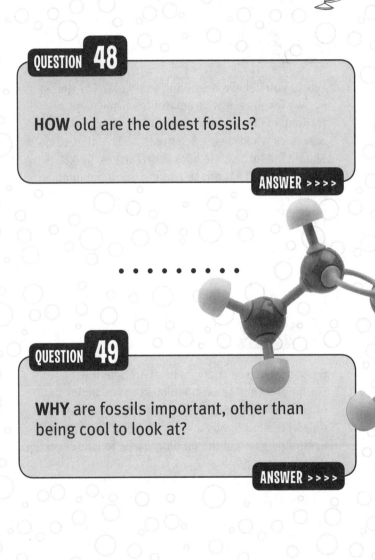

QUESTION 49

WHY are fossils important, other than being cool to look at?

ANSWER > > > >

OUTSMART SCIENCE

ANSWER 48

Would you believe 3.5 billion years old? The oldest
known fossils are of stromatolites. They were
trapped in once-gooey sheets of cyanobacteria,
way back when. Some scientists believe that some
simple life forms date back even farther, to 3.8
billion years. That doesn't sound like a big jump,
from 3.5 to 3.8 billion, until you realize .3 billion
adds another 300 million years to the equation.

• • • • • • • •

ANSWER 49

Fossils let us see changes in environmental
conditions and life over millions or even billions
of years. They can help scientists discover the
date of the era or epoch when the fossil originally
lived. And some of the medium-sized fossils make
great doorstops.

QUESTION 50

WHAT do you call people who study fossils?

ANSWER > > > >

• • • • • • • • •

QUESTION 51

WHAT system do scientists use in determining the age of a fossil or other geological specimen?

ANSWER > > > >

ANSWER 50

You probably call them paleontologists, unless they're your Aunt Betty and Uncle Gene. Then you call them Aunt Betty and Uncle Gene. You may be thinking that paleontologists only study dinosaurs. No, they study all the old fossils. But dinosaurs are the "big time" of paleontology.

• • • • • • • • •

ANSWER 51

They use radioactive dating. The best-known form of radioactive dating is carbon-14 dating.

QUESTION 52

WHAT is carbon-14 dating?

ANSWER > > > >

· · · · · · · · ·

QUESTION 53

WHAT (besides radioactive dating) gives important clues about the Earth's history?

ANSWER > > > >

ANSWER 52

Carbon-14 (radioactive) dating tells you when something died. Basically, all living things are mostly made of carbon. Some of this carbon is C-14. When the organism dies, its C-14 starts disintegrating at a predictable rate. Scientists simply measure how much C-14 is left, do some math, and then come up with an answer like "23 thousand years old." It's that easy.

• • • • • • • •

ANSWER 53

Geologic layers give plenty of evidence to geologists, paleontologists, and well-diggers. Each geologic period left its own unique debris, with ice ages in between leaving "lines" like the rings of a tree.

QUESTION 54

HOW long has there been life on Earth?

ANSWER > > > >

• • • • • • • • •

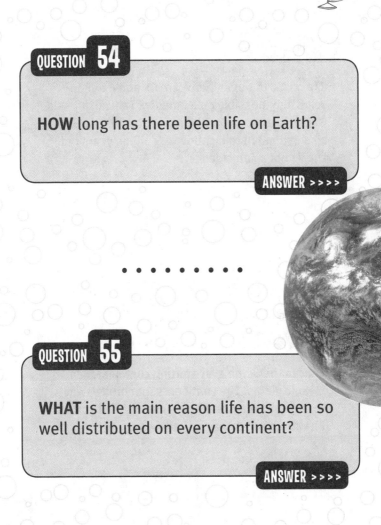

QUESTION 55

WHAT is the main reason life has been so well distributed on every continent?

ANSWER > > > >

ANSWER 54

Life on Earth began between 3.5 and 4 billion years ago, possibly on a Monday. The Earth itself is estimated to be 4.5 billion years old. The Sun is also estimated to be about 4.5 billion years old. This is not a coincidence.

• • • • • • • • •

ANSWER 55

You can thank the ever-shifting continental and oceanic plates. The continents that broke away from the main mass (Eurasia) brought all sorts of life with them as they drifted away.

QUESTION 56

WHAT is an ice age?

ANSWER > > > >

· · · · · · · · · ·

QUESTION 57

WHEN did the most recent ice age begin and end?

ANSWER > > > >

ANSWER 56

An ice age is a long period of below-freezing temperatures. The result: Continental ice sheets and polar ice sheets expanded, and mountain glaciers came to town.

• • • • • • • •

ANSWER 57

The most recent ice age ended about 12,000 years ago. It began about 72,000 years ago. In the United States it's called the Wisconsin glaciation, and in England it's the Devensian glaciation. Either way, it was cold.

QUESTION **58**

WHAT was the impact of the last ice age on animal life?

ANSWER > > > >

· · · · · · · · ·

QUESTION **59**

WHEN is the next ice age coming?

ANSWER > > > >

OUTSMART SCIENCE

ANSWER 58

There was a mass extinction of many birds and
large mammals, including saber-toothed cats,
giant sloths, mammoths, mastodons, and other
big beasts known scientifically as Pleistocene
megafauna and, informally, as "big scary things."

• • • • • • • • •

ANSWER 59

Yes, there will be a next one. Ice ages generally
occur every 40,000 years, though the last few
occurred after 100,000-year intervals. So we can
safely guess the next big chill will be between
30,000 and 90,000 years from now. For the record,
this epoch between ice ages is called MIS-1, or the
Flandrian interglacial, if you're British. Either way,
it's a lot warmer than an ice age.

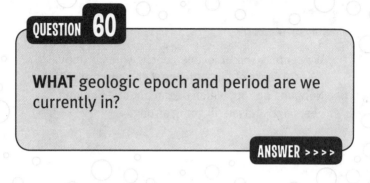

QUESTION 60

WHAT geologic epoch and period are we currently in?

ANSWER >>>>

• • • • • • • • •

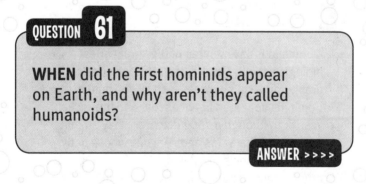

QUESTION 61

WHEN did the first hominids appear on Earth, and why aren't they called humanoids?

ANSWER >>>>

ANSWER 60

Welcome to the Holocene epoch, which is about 12,000 years old. It's the most current part of the Neogene period, which began about 23 million years ago and is still going strong.

• • • • • • • • •

ANSWER 61

A hominid is any member of the "great apes" biological family (hominidae). This includes gorillas, orangutans, chimpanzees, and all you humans. Hominids appeared between four and five million years ago (though a 2002 discovery may up that to seven million years ago). Anyone whose body resembles a human is a humanoid, including aliens, robots, and our hairy ancestors. But that's much more a term of science fiction than science fact.

QUESTION 62

WHEN did the first actual humans appear on Earth?

ANSWER > > > >

• • • • • • • • •

QUESTION 63

WHAT single factor has the most influence on shaping Earth's landscape?

ANSWER > > > >

ANSWER 62

The first humans (*Homo sapiens*) reported for duty between 1.6 and 2 million years ago, depending on which websites you frequent. And, because we never shy away from controversy, we'd like to report that our closest living relative is the chimpanzee.

• • • • • • • • •

ANSWER 63

Water—especially water moving downhill. The wash of water across land continues to shape mountains, move rock, dig canyons, create lakes, help rivers grow, irrigate land, distribute soil, and much more.

QUESTION 64

WHAT percentage of Earth's surface is covered by water?

ANSWER >>>>

• • • • • • • • •

QUESTION 65

WHAT is the average depth of the ocean?

ANSWER >>>>

ANSWER **64**

About three-fourths of Earth (between 70 and 75 percent) is under the wet stuff, including the slowly melting ice caps.

• • • • • • • • •

ANSWER **65**

The average ocean depth is 2.35 miles (12,408 feet, or about 10 Empire State Buildings tip to tail).

QUESTION 66

WHERE is the world's deepest spot?

ANSWER > > > >

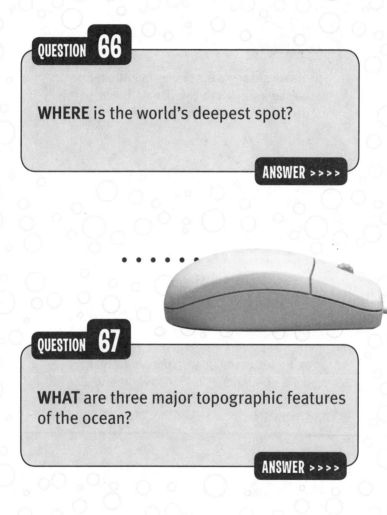

QUESTION 67

WHAT are three major topographic features of the ocean?

ANSWER > > > >

ANSWER 66

The deepest spot is 6.78 miles (35,800 feet) below sea level. It's the Marianas Trench, in the northwest Pacific, not far from Japan.

• • • • • • • • •

ANSWER 67

Down under, ocean floors, continental margins, and mid-ocean ridges rule. Above ground, Earth's topographic features include mountains, canyons, and flatlands.

QUESTION **68**

HOW do you rank Earth's oceans, from biggest to smallest?

ANSWER > > > >

. . . .

QUESTION **69**

HOW has climate determined the way organisms are distributed throughout the planet?

ANSWER > > > >

ANSWER 68

(1) Pacific, (2) Atlantic, (3) Indian, (4) Antarctic, and
(5) Arctic. The Arctic Ocean is the one that surrounds the
North Pole. The Antarctic Ocean hugs the South Pole.

• • • • • • • • •

ANSWER 69

Organisms, like everyone else, like to go where there's
food, habitat, and a chance for survival. And anyone,
even an organism, is going to thrive where the climate
is hospitable. A look at Earth's climate zones reveals the
greatest abundance and diversity of organisms in the
most hospitable (read: pleasant) climates.

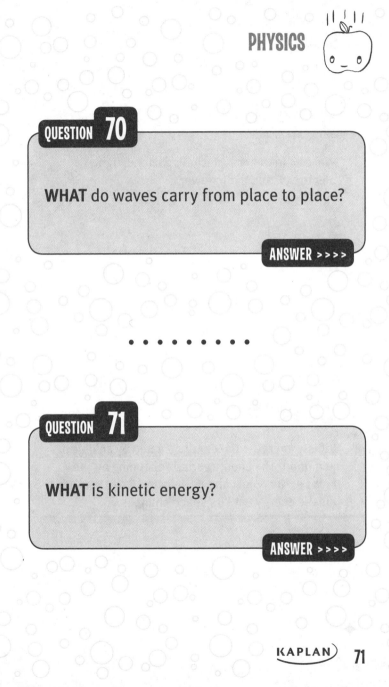

QUESTION 70

WHAT do waves carry from place to place?

ANSWER > > > >

• • • • • • • • •

QUESTION 71

WHAT is kinetic energy?

ANSWER > > > >

ANSWER 70

Waves carry energy, including sound, light, electricity, and hydropower.

• • • • • • • • •

ANSWER 71

Kinetic energy is the energy created by an object in motion. The energy varies depending on the mass of the object and its velocity. It will keep its kinetic energy until its speed changes.

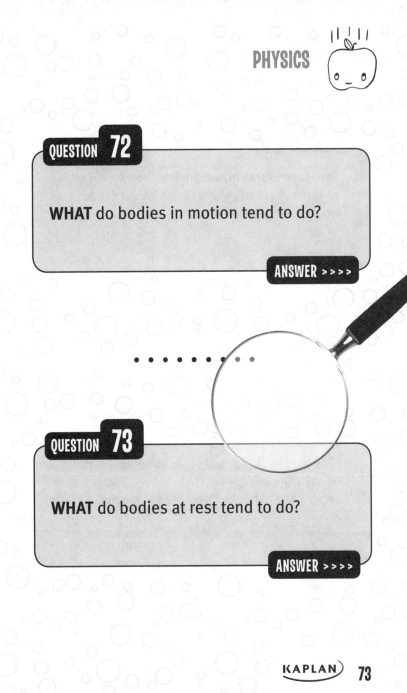

QUESTION 72

WHAT do bodies in motion tend to do?

ANSWER > > > >

QUESTION 73

WHAT do bodies at rest tend to do?

ANSWER > > > >

They tend to stay in motion, until something acts on them (meaning, stops them). This is called Newton's first law of motion.

• • • • • • • • •

They tend to stay at rest, until something acts on them (meaning, gets them going). This is the second half of Newton's first law of motion.

QUESTION 74

WHAT is the result of every action, at least as far as Newton's third law of motion goes?

ANSWER >>>>

• • • • • • • •

QUESTION 75

HOW much energy is needed to return a body in motion back to a state of rest—more, less, or the same amount of energy needed for acceleration?

ANSWER >>>>

ANSWER 74

For every action, there is an equal and opposite reaction. A pool cue hitting a billiard ball is a good example of this law of motion.

. . . .

ANSWER 75

Twice as much, actually. No matter what speed you are traveling at, you need to use (or lose) twice as much energy to stop.

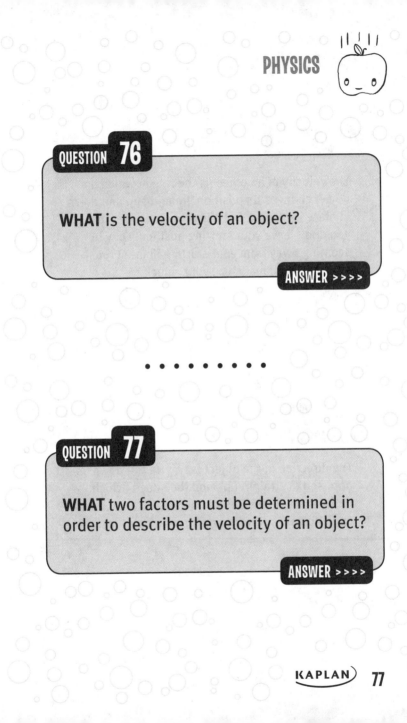

QUESTION **76**

WHAT is the velocity of an object?

ANSWER >>>>

• • • • • • • •

QUESTION **77**

WHAT two factors must be determined in order to describe the velocity of an object?

ANSWER >>>>

ANSWER 76

The velocity of an object is the rate at which an object changes its position. Jumping up and down in place is motion, but it isn't velocity, because you don't leave your starting position. Only by scooting away from your starting point at top speed will you maximize your velocity.

• • • • • • • • •

ANSWER 77

The direction of the object (say, straight down as opposed to straight up), and the speed (which, for instance, increases when going straight down, and decreases when going straight up).

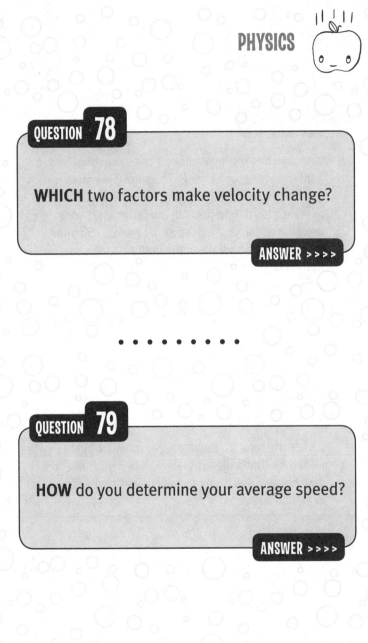

QUESTION **78**

WHICH two factors make velocity change?

ANSWER > > > >

• • • • • • • •

QUESTION **79**

HOW do you determine your average speed?

ANSWER > > > >

ANSWER 78

Velocity changes if you make a change in direction (a hard right turn) or a change in speed (slamming on the brakes), or both (you slam on the brakes before making a hard right turn). In the latter case, your wheels squeal, you kick up some gravel, and your velocity decreases; when the police do the same thing, your velocity increases again—tell them it's your physics homework that made you do it.

• • • • • • • • •

ANSWER 79

Divide the total distance you've traveled by the total time that's elapsed. Remember, your speed may have varied along the way. That's why it's called an average.

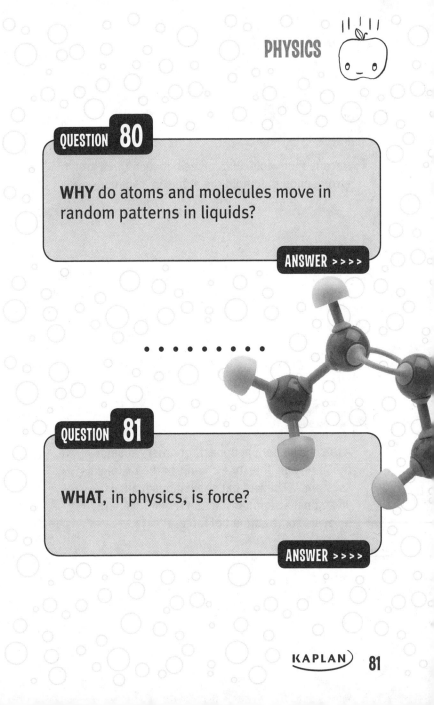

QUESTION 80

WHY do atoms and molecules move in random patterns in liquids?

ANSWER > > > >

• • • • • • • • •

QUESTION 81

WHAT, in physics, is force?

ANSWER > > > >

ANSWER 80

Because the molecular forces between them aren't strong enough to hold the atoms in a solid form.

• • • • • • • • •

ANSWER 81

A force is an action, impact, or other cause that's responsible for a change in the recipient's "system." (Think of bat against baseball, or yo-yo against string.) Any action requiring energy involves some amount of force.

QUESTION **82**

WHAT are the two kinds of forces?

ANSWER >>>>

• • • • • • • • •

QUESTION **83**

WHAT two characteristics are always present in force?

ANSWER >>>>

ANSWER 82

There are contact forces and field forces. When one object has physical contact with another (finger against doorbell or air into balloon), that's contact force. On the other hand, magnets and gravity are field forces. No contact is necessary.

• • • • • • • • •

ANSWER 83

For a force to be a force, it needs to have direction (so that it can get to the thing it's going to affect) and magnitude (the ability to actually make an impact on something else).

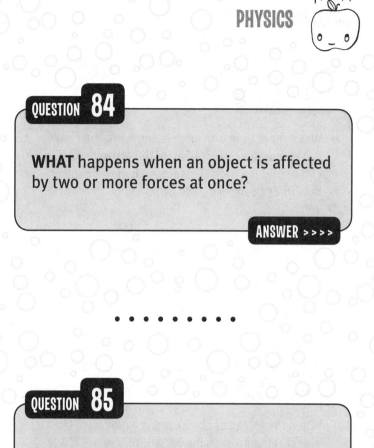

QUESTION 84

WHAT happens when an object is affected by two or more forces at once?

ANSWER > > > >

• • • • • • • • •

QUESTION 85

WHAT happens when the forces on an object are balanced?

ANSWER > > > >

ANSWER 84

When more than one force is with you, the result is a cumulative effect of all of the forces. Imagine you're under a rock avalanche. Then you can see how forces can really add up.

• • • • • • • • •

ANSWER 85

When the forces are balanced the motion of the object remains unchanged, whether or not it was moving at the time of impact.

QUESTION 86

WHAT happens when the forces on an object are unbalanced?

ANSWER > > > >

• • • • • • • •

QUESTION 87

WHEN the mass of an object increases, does it require more or less force to remain in motion at the same speed?

ANSWER > > > >

The velocity of the object will change—faster or slower, and it changes direction, too. May the forces be with you.

· · · · · · · ·

More. More. More. More. More. Picture six more clowns piled into a little car already filled with clowns—the car's engine would require a lot more force to get them to the circus on time.

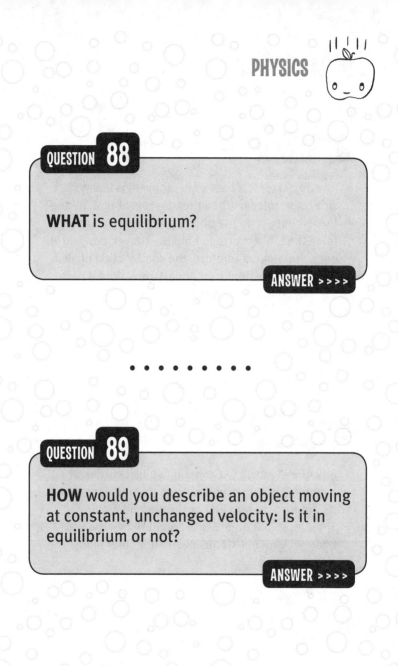

QUESTION **88**

WHAT is equilibrium?

ANSWER > > > >

• • • • • • • • •

QUESTION **89**

HOW would you describe an object moving at constant, unchanged velocity: Is it in equilibrium or not?

ANSWER > > > >

Any object (say, a bust of Beethoven) is always subject to forces. When the object is at rest, all the forces that act on the object (the gravity and the force the table exerts to hold Beethoven up) cancel each other out. Therefore, the combination of all the forces (the net force) equals zero. With a net force of zero, you've got equilibrium.

• • • • • • • • •

ANSWER **89**

Any object moving at constant velocity (think of a meteor) is not accelerating or slowing down, so its net force is zero just as if it weren't moving. Therefore, that object is in equilibrium. Now you know why rolling stones need not gather moss.

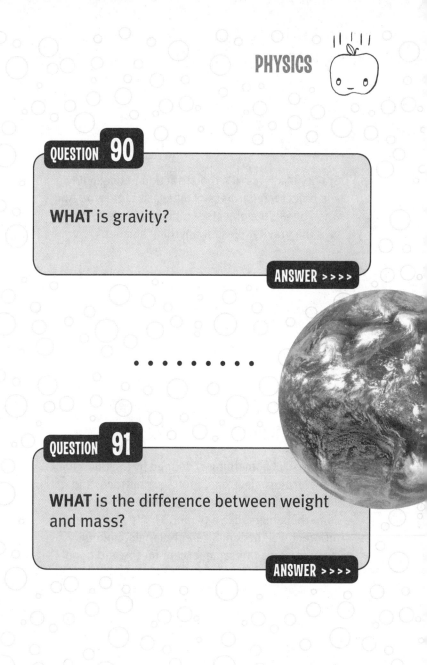

QUESTION 90

WHAT is gravity?

ANSWER > > > >

• • • • • • • • •

QUESTION 91

WHAT is the difference between weight and mass?

ANSWER > > > >

ANSWER 90

Gravity is a force. It's the attraction between any two objects, regardless of mass, size, or form. And when one of the objects is a planet, it pretty much sets the gravity rules for anything smaller.

• • • • • • • • •

ANSWER 91

The mass of something is defined by the quantity of molecules, electrons, protons, neutrons, and so on. Weight is relative to the attraction force of something huge, like a planet. That's why we have different weights on different planets, but our mass remains the same (except for the additional space suit).

WHY is the Moon's gravity less than Earth's?

ANSWER > > > >

• • • • • • • • •

WHAT does a 100-pound person weigh on Jupiter?

ANSWER > > > >

ANSWER 92

It's not really because the Moon is smaller than the Earth. It has more to do with Earth having more mass and therefore a greater gravitational effect. The gravity on the Moon is about one-sixth of Earth's, which means you 200-pounders would weigh 34 pounds. That's quite a jump.

• • • • • • • •

ANSWER 93

Jupiter's gravity is 2.54 times greater than Earth's gravity. So, a 100-pounder would weigh 254 pounds and would move slowly, too. Interestingly (for some), Jupiter's mass is actually 317 times the mass of Earth, but due to some complicated math, you wouldn't weigh 31,700 pounds if you visited. You'd never leave.

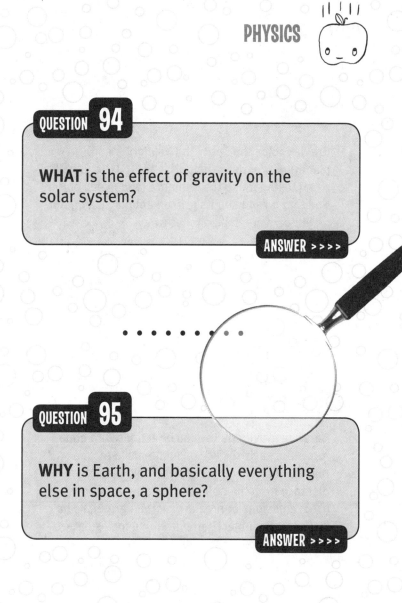

QUESTION 94

WHAT is the effect of gravity on the solar system?

ANSWER > > > >

QUESTION 95

WHY is Earth, and basically everything else in space, a sphere?

ANSWER > > > >

ANSWER 94

Gravity holds the Earth and its eight (or so) planetary friends in their orbit around the Sun. It's a real testimony to the influence (and mass) of the Sun that it can keep its grip on not only Earth, but on Pluto, over a billion miles away.

• • • • • • • •

ANSWER 95

Because gravity pulls in all directions with equal force. So, each surface on an object (a rock, a planet, etc.) will ultimately end up the same distance from the object's core. Any variations (from collisions or breakaways) will gradually be forced by the object's gravitational forces back into the shape of a sphere.

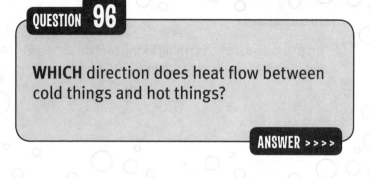

QUESTION **96**

WHICH direction does heat flow between cold things and hot things?

ANSWER > > > >

• • • • • • • •

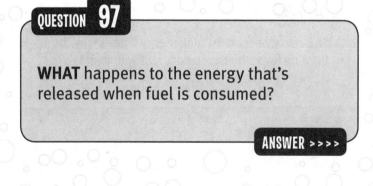

QUESTION **97**

WHAT happens to the energy that's released when fuel is consumed?

ANSWER > > > >

ANSWER **96**

Heat flows from the hot thing to the cold thing until they're equally warm things.

• • • • • • • •

ANSWER **97**

The energy becomes heat energy. That's why the burning logs, the car engine, and your average flamethrower are hot.

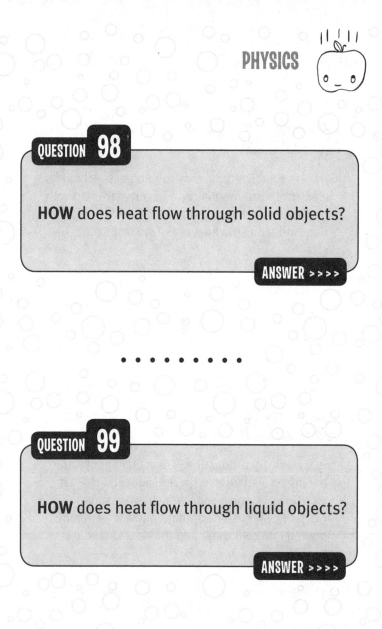

QUESTION 98

HOW does heat flow through solid objects?

ANSWER > > > >

• • • • • • • • • •

QUESTION 99

HOW does heat flow through liquid objects?

ANSWER > > > >

ANSWER 98

Heat is conducted through solid objects—it is transmitted across matter, without matter actually flowing through those objects. Think of a metal pot conducting the heat of the stove it's on.

• • • • • • • • •

ANSWER 99

Two ways. By conduction—think of a pot of water boiling on a stove (see previous question). Heat also flows by convection, which is a result of matter flowing. Think of that boiling water being poured into cold water and the heat spreading.

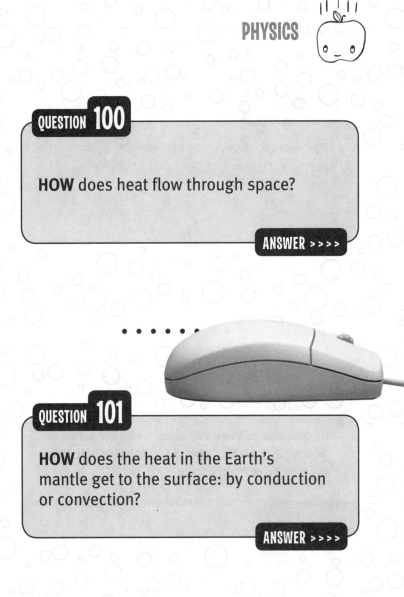

QUESTION 100

HOW does heat flow through space?

ANSWER > > > >

QUESTION 101

HOW does the heat in the Earth's mantle get to the surface: by conduction or convection?

ANSWER > > > >

ANSWER 100

By radiation. It can radiate from the Sun, 93 million miles away, or from a lightbulb on your desk. Don't touch!

• • • • • • • • •

ANSWER 101

By convection. It flows upward toward the surface, mostly via red-hot magma. Magma either boils the water or bubbles up as lava.

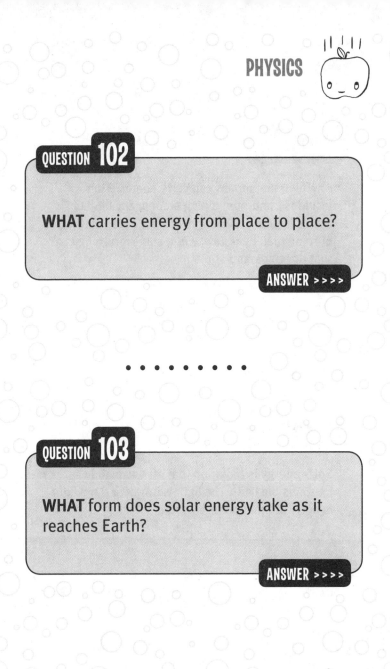

QUESTION **102**

WHAT carries energy from place to place?

ANSWER > > > >

• • • • • • • • •

QUESTION **103**

WHAT form does solar energy take as it reaches Earth?

ANSWER > > > >

ANSWER 102

Anything that moves can carry energy. That includes raindrops, rolling stones, any kind of waves (sound waves, light waves, ocean waves), burning fuel, heat flow, wind, and everything else that doesn't stand still.

• • • • • • • •

ANSWER 103

Solar energy is radiation that arrives mainly as light. Visible light. The light is bright and the light is hot, but first and foremost, it's light.

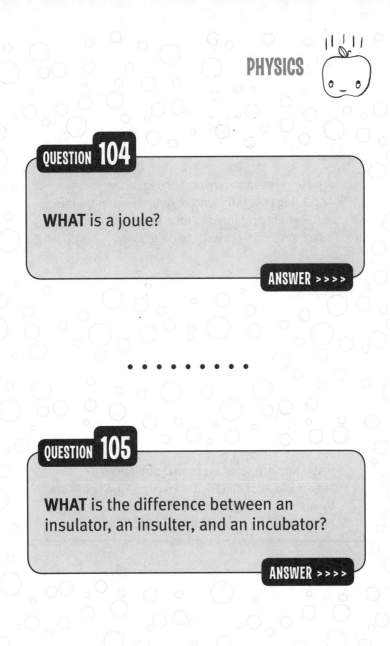

QUESTION 104

WHAT is a joule?

ANSWER > > > >

• • • • • • • • • •

QUESTION 105

WHAT is the difference between an insulator, an insulter, and an incubator?

ANSWER > > > >

A joule is the standard unit of heat energy. According to legend (and several websites), a joule is the energy required to lift a small, 3.5 oz. apple 3 feet in the air against Earth's gravity.

• • • • • • • • •

Insulators are substances that don't easily conduct heat or electricity. Insulters don't conduct themselves nicely in public. Incubators conduct eggs into chicks using heat and light.

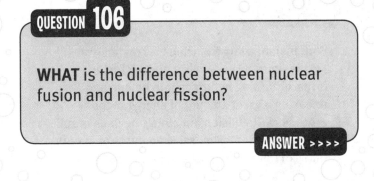

QUESTION **106**

WHAT is the difference between nuclear fusion and nuclear fission?

ANSWER > > > >

• • • • • • • • •

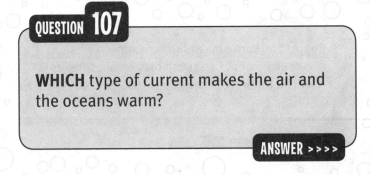

QUESTION **107**

WHICH type of current makes the air and the oceans warm?

ANSWER > > > >

ANSWER **106**

With fusion, a larger nucleus is created from smaller ones. (The Sun is a nuclear fusion furnace, turning hydrogen into helium and releasing a great amount of energy in the process.) With fission, an atom's nucleus is split apart. (This creates massive amounts of energy that can power a city, or even a submarine.)

• • • • • • • • •

ANSWER **107**

Convection currents. While the warmer air rises and cooler air falls, the wind they create spreads warm air throughout the geosphere.

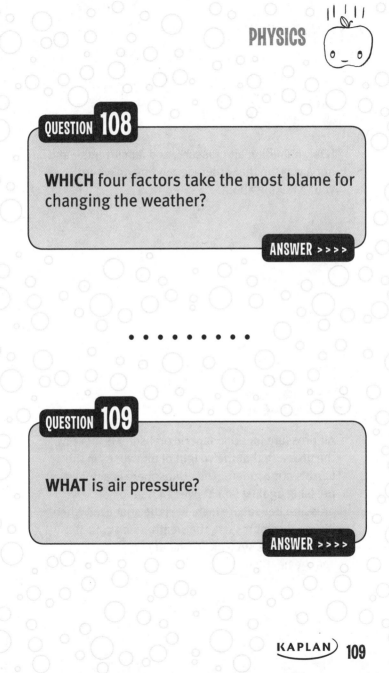

QUESTION **108**

WHICH four factors take the most blame for changing the weather?

ANSWER > > > >

• • • • • • • • •

QUESTION **109**

WHAT is air pressure?

ANSWER > > > >

ANSWER 108

Heat, humidity, air pressure, and air currents—and not always in that order, depending on where you're talking about.

• • • • • • • • •

ANSWER 109

Air pressure (or atmospheric pressure) is literally the pressure that the weight of air causes in the Earth's atmosphere. The atmosphere is actually pressing against you at over 14 pounds of pressure per square inch. Feel the squeeze? When it's most compressed, the weatherman calls it a high pressure system. To find out what you call it, see the next question.

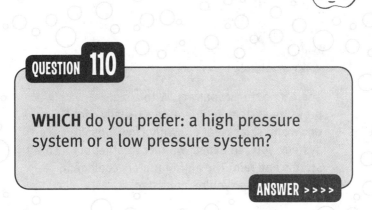

QUESTION 110

WHICH do you prefer: a high pressure system or a low pressure system?

ANSWER >>>>

• • • • • • • • • •

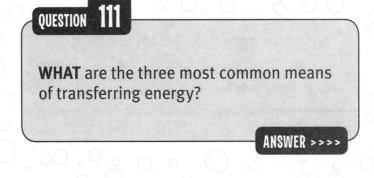

QUESTION 111

WHAT are the three most common means of transferring energy?

ANSWER >>>>

There's no correct answer. With a high pressure system, temperatures usually cool down and skies clear up. With a low pressure system, you can expect warmer weather but also storms and rain. The author prefers cooler and sunnier, in case you're interested.

• • • • • • • • •

Convection, conduction, and radiation.

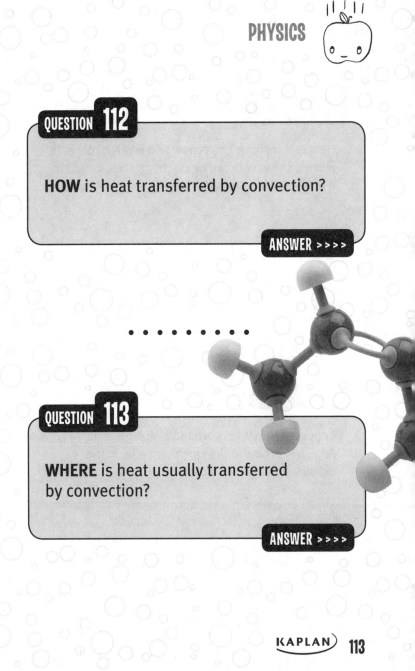

QUESTION 112

HOW is heat transferred by convection?

ANSWER > > > >

• • • • • • • • •

QUESTION 113

WHERE is heat usually transferred by convection?

ANSWER > > > >

ANSWER 112

Heat is transferred by convection when it comes in waves. The waves can be electric waves, or within a fluid, or the result of force.

• • • • • • • • •

ANSWER 113

Convection heat gets around everywhere: It regularly occurs in the Earth's mantle, in the oceans, and in the atmosphere.

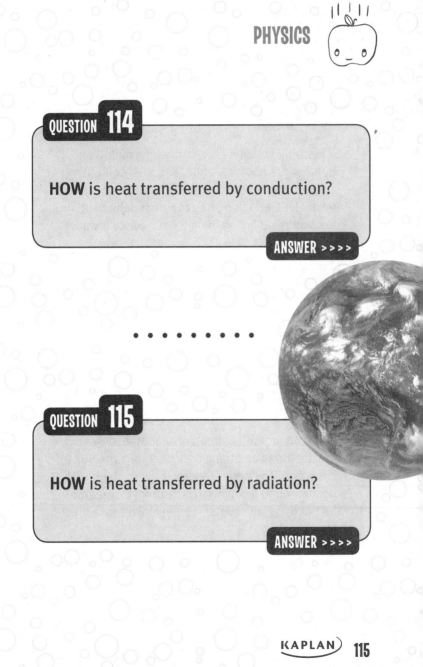

QUESTION 114

HOW is heat transferred by conduction?

ANSWER > > > >

• • • • • • • • • •

QUESTION 115

HOW is heat transferred by radiation?

ANSWER > > > >

ANSWER 114

Something gets hot (say, something metal) and then it stays hot for a while, and then something touches it (say, your hand) and that gets hot, too. Voila! The metal thing has conducted the heat. And now you're reversing the effect under cold water.

• • • • • • • • •

ANSWER 115

Radiation, or radiant heat, is heat that comes directly from something that's hot, like the Sun (or a radiator). The hotter the hot thing is, the hotter the air around it will be. The farther you are from the hot thing, the cooler it gets. Make sense?

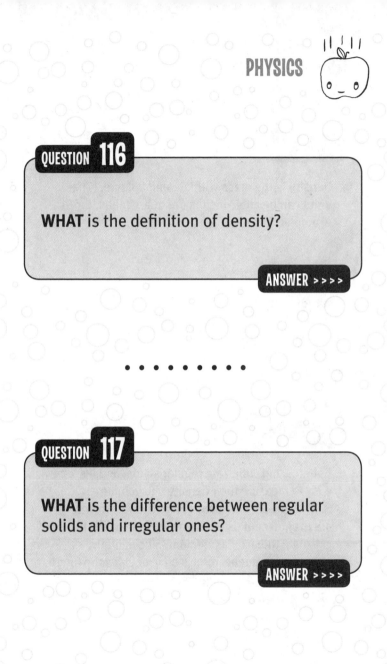

QUESTION 116

WHAT is the definition of density?

ANSWER > > > >

• • • • • • • • •

QUESTION 117

WHAT is the difference between regular solids and irregular ones?

ANSWER > > > >

ANSWER 116

Density is the mass within a unit volume. (The units can be cubic inches or square miles, for example.) The more mass, the more dense.

• • • • • • • • •

ANSWER 117

Spheres and cubes are regular solids, and it's easy to measure their density and volume. Snakes, trees, philosophers, and royal crowns are irregular solids. It takes a lot more math to calculate those measurements. Incidentally, a hebesphenomegacorona is an irregular solid figure with 21 faces (18 triangular, the other 3 square), looking like a golf ball shaved by a hatchet.

QUESTION 118

WHY do air bubbles rise?

ANSWER > > > >

• • • • • • • • • •

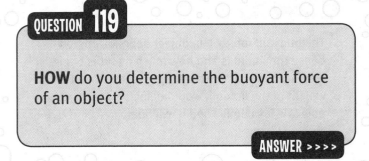

QUESTION 119

HOW do you determine the buoyant force of an object?

ANSWER > > > >

ANSWER **118**

As you learned in your first bathtub, bubbles rise to the surface. The air in those bubbles is displacing (or shoving aside) the water it's next to. But the water doesn't want to be shoved aside. So it shoves back with equal force and squeezes the bubbles to the top. The measurable force of that water shoving back is called buoyant force.

• • • • • • • • •

ANSWER **119**

The buoyant force of an object depends on how dense the liquid is and how much liquid is being displaced. If the object's weight is less than the weight of the liquid it would displace, then the object is less dense and it will float.

QUESTION 120

WHAT are some of the key effects of gravity here on Earth?

ANSWER >>>>

• • • • • • • •

QUESTION 121

WHAT makes the wind blow: gravity, the Sun, or the Moon?

ANSWER >>>>

ANSWER 120

Gravity keeps the Earth's atmosphere, oceans, and inhabitants from drifting into space. Gravity pulls the rain to the rivers and ultimately to the sea. Gravity guides the development and growth of plants and affects the way our bones and muscles develop and function. And gravity keeps us from floating out of convertible cars.

• • • • • • • •

ANSWER 121

The Sun is the one. Heated air rises, and cooler air falls in the process called convection. This ongoing up-and-down activity causes the back-and-forth action we call wind.

QUESTION 122

WHAT are the "building blocks of life" in all living organisms actually called?

ANSWER >>>>

· · · · · · · · ·

QUESTION 123

HOW many cells do you have to have to respectably call yourself an organism?

ANSWER >>>>

ANSWER 122

They're called cells. However, being in a "cell block for life" is a whole different matter.

• • • • • • • •

ANSWER 123

One is enough. The amoeba and bacteria are single-celled, but they're definitely players.

QUESTION 124

HOW many cells are in the average human?

ANSWER >>>>

• • • • • • • • •

QUESTION 125

WHAT is directly in front of you if you are looking at a red blood cell?

ANSWER >>>>

ANSWER 124

100 trillion. Or 10^{14}. Or a lot.

• • • • • • • •

ANSWER 125

A microscope. A red blood cell is about 20 micrometers across, or about one-tenth the width of a human hair.

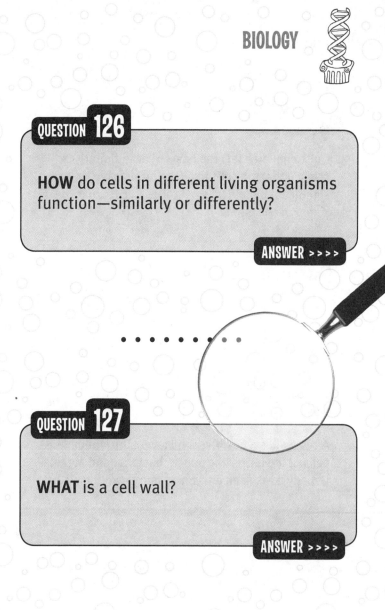

QUESTION **126**

HOW do cells in different living organisms function—similarly or differently?

ANSWER > > > >

QUESTION **127**

WHAT is a cell wall?

ANSWER > > > >

ANSWER 126

Quite similarly. It is the basis of evolutionary science that the cells in all life forms have significant biological similarities due to their common ancestry.

• • • • • • • • •

ANSWER 127

A cell wall is a flexible, solid layer surrounding the cells of life forms like plants, bacteria, and algae. Usually it takes an enzyme to tear down the wall.

QUESTION **128**

WHAT do plant cells have that animal cells don't?

ANSWER >>>>

• • • • • • • • •

QUESTION **129**

WHAT is a cell membrane?

ANSWER >>>>

ANSWER 128

Plant cells have a cell wall, chloroplasts, and larger vacuoles. Plant cells are also more rectangular because their cell walls are more rigid.

• • • • • • • • •

ANSWER 129

We animals have cell membranes instead of cell walls, but they do the same job. The plasma membrane separates and protects a cell from its surrounding environment. If you're interested (and if you're not), they're largely made from lipids.

QUESTION **130**

WHAT is the outside "skin" of an animal cell called?

ANSWER > > > >

• • • • • • • • •

QUESTION **131**

WHAT is the nucleus of a cell?

ANSWER > > > >

It's a semipermeable membrane. It regulates the ways a cell interacts with its environment, and it keeps the cell's tiny parts from wandering. (FYI, the name Semipermeable Membrane is still available for your garage rock band.)

• • • • • • • • •

The nucleus is the part of the cell that is responsible for growth, storing genetic information, and reproduction. If you're looking for a reproduction joke here, forget it.

QUESTION **132**

WHAT are organelles?

ANSWER > > > >

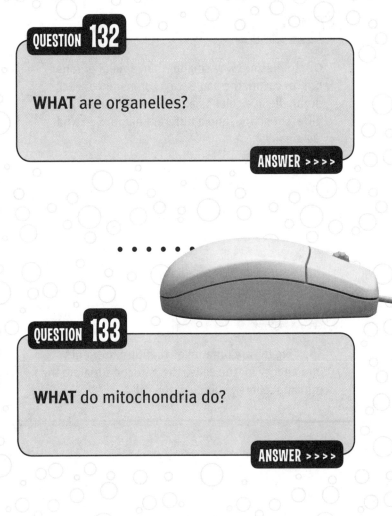

QUESTION **133**

WHAT do mitochondria do?

ANSWER > > > >

Organelles are way smaller than animal organs, but they work the same way. For instance, each organelle in a cell has a different function, a different shape, and a different name. See what we mean?

. . . .

The "big m" are organelles that turn nutrients into energy for the cells. The mitochondria are the principal energy source of the cell.

QUESTION 134

WHERE do cells come from?

ANSWER > > > >

• • • • • • • •

QUESTION 135

HOW do cells increase their population?

ANSWER > > > >

OUTSMART SCIENCE

ANSWER 134

From a parent cell splitting in half. Yes, sir, that's mitosis. And it is understood that all cells on Earth come from a single source. Therefore, way, way back, there was just one cell. Where it came from is the source of all kinds of debates.

• • • • • • • • •

ANSWER 135

Through mitosis, when they divide.

QUESTION 136

WHAT are the daughter cells?

ANSWER > > > >

• • • • • • • • •

QUESTION 137

WHEN daughter cells grow up to become parent cells, can they divide again?

ANSWER > > > >

ANSWER 136

They're the twin result of mitosis—identical cells with identical sets of chromosomes that come from the parent cell. You could say that mitosis is splitting up for the sake of the kids.

. . . .

ANSWER 137

Yes—mitosis is not only ongoing, it's the basis of the continuance of life. Remember, all cells exist because of cell division.

QUESTION 138

WHEN multicellular organisms develop, what happens to all their multicells?

ANSWER >>>>

· · · · · · · · · ·

QUESTION 139

WHY are cells called "cells"?

ANSWER >>>>

ANSWER 138

They differentiate, which means they go through the normal process of maturing, which means they can do the jobs they're supposed to do.

• • • • • • • • •

ANSWER 139

Because back in 1665, British scientist Robert Hooke stared at a cork through an ancient microscope, saw the honeycomb of cells, and thought they looked like the small dormitory cells where monks slept in monasteries.

QUESTION **140**

WHAT is a cytoskeleton?

ANSWER > > > >

• • • • • • • • •

QUESTION **141**

WHERE is genetic information in a cell found?

ANSWER > > > >

ANSWER 140

A cytoskeleton helps the cell keep its shape and its contents in order. Think of a gooey plastic bag. To a cell, that's a skeleton.

• • • • • • • • •

ANSWER 141

In the nucleus, remember? We told you that a few answers ago.

WHAT is the importance of a cell's genetic instructions?

ANSWER > > > >

· · · · · · · · ·

WHAT can affect traits beside the genetic instructions?

ANSWER > > > >

ANSWER **142**

They specify the traits of the cell. Traits are everything you inherited from Mom and Dad, especially how you look. From hair color to toe length, you can't trade your traits.

• • • • • • • • •

ANSWER **143**

Environmental influences. For instance, if you grow up in a jungle and your identical twin grows up in Antarctica, you will each look quite different at your 50th birthday reunion.

QUESTION 144

HOW do sexually reproduced organisms get their genes?

ANSWER > > > >

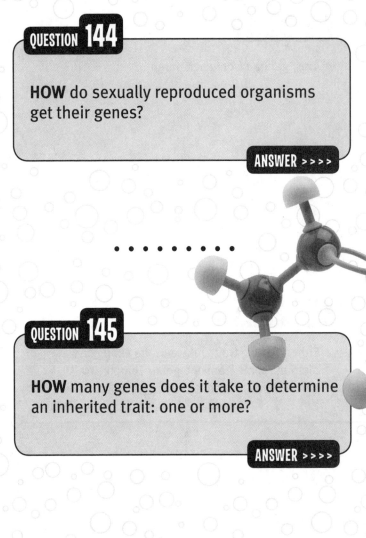

QUESTION 145

HOW many genes does it take to determine an inherited trait: one or more?

ANSWER > > > >

They get half from each parent.

· · · · · · · · ·

Either. Simple traits, like earlobe shape and dimples, come from one gene. Complex traits, like behavior, come from multiple genes.

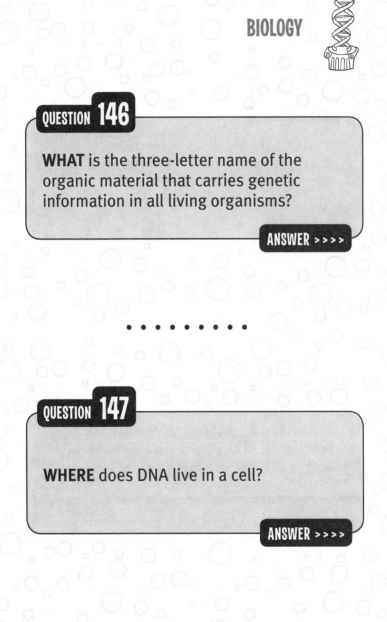

QUESTION 146

WHAT is the three-letter name of the organic material that carries genetic information in all living organisms?

ANSWER >>>>

• • • • • • • • •

QUESTION 147

WHERE does DNA live in a cell?

ANSWER >>>>

ANSWER 146

It's DNA, to be precise. Its full name is deoxyribonucleic acid, so if you were being really precise, its initials would be DORNA.

• • • • • • • • •

ANSWER 147

In the chromosomes. They're big molecules (macromolecules, actually) that have the job of holding all the genetic information together.

QUESTION 148

HOW many copies of each gene do plants, animals, and middle-school students have?

ANSWER >>>>

• • • • • • • • • •

QUESTION 149

WHAT are the set of copies of genes called?

ANSWER >>>>

ANSWER 148

Two copies. One from each parent. Incidentally, they may not be identical.

• • • • • • • • •

ANSWER 149

Alleles (uh-LEELS).

QUESTION 150

WHICH genes in an allele get their traits passed along, and which don't?

ANSWER > > > >

• • • • • • • •

QUESTION 151

WHAT is the term for gradual change among a species?

ANSWER > > > >

ANSWER 150

Dominant genes get passed along, while recessive genes don't. And then suddenly, after 11 generations or so, 2 recessive genes team up, and a blue-eyed kid shows up in a brown-eyed family.

• • • • • • • •

ANSWER 151

Evolution, my dear Watson!

QUESTION 152

WHO is the scientist who discovered evolution?

ANSWER > > > >

• • • • • • • • •

QUESTION 153

WHAT can cause a species to evolve quickly?

ANSWER > > > >

ANSWER 152

A naturalist named Charles Darwin. In 1831, he
went sailing to the isolated Galapagos Islands,
saw the diversity that nature is capable of, and got
to thinking.

· · · · · · · · ·

ANSWER 153

Mutation. If a much larger offspring appears,
say, and begins to pass that trait along to its
descendants, then height will have evolved in
that species.

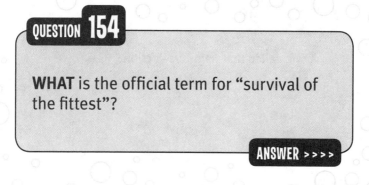

QUESTION 154

WHAT is the official term for "survival of the fittest"?

ANSWER > > > >

• • • • • • • •

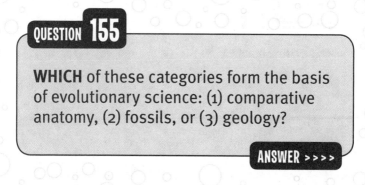

QUESTION 155

WHICH of these categories form the basis of evolutionary science: (1) comparative anatomy, (2) fossils, or (3) geology?

ANSWER > > > >

Darwin called that natural selection.

All of the above.

HOW are shared, derived, and observable characteristics of living organisms handy to scientists?

ANSWER > > > >

WHICH three choices are available to an organism whose environment has just changed?

ANSWER > > > >

They help scientists group and classify organisms by species, genus, and so on up the ladder.

• • • • • • • •

Adapt, leave, or die.

QUESTION **158**

WHAT is the usual cause for a species' extinction?

ANSWER > > > >

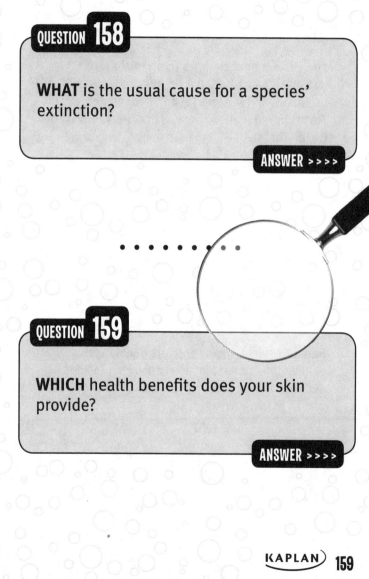

QUESTION **159**

WHICH health benefits does your skin provide?

ANSWER > > > >

ANSWER 158

The environment changes (perhaps because of a glacier, or a lack of food, or a hungry new predator), and the species can't adequately adapt. This is infrequently known as the "un-survival" of the un-fittest.

• • • • • • • •

ANSWER 159

Skin is a shield, giving you lots of defenses against infection. Skin also keeps your insides in and the outside out.

QUESTION 160

WHAT on Earth is the biosphere?

ANSWER >>>>

• • • • • • • • •

QUESTION 161

WHAT on Earth is the hydrosphere?

ANSWER >>>>

ANSWER 160

The biosphere is every part of the planet where life occurs.

. . . .

ANSWER 161

The hydrosphere is every part of the planet that's filled with water.

BIOLOGY

QUESTION 162

WHICH kind of system is a river: static or dynamic?

ANSWER > > > >

• • • • • • • • • •

QUESTION 163

HOW can the Earth change a habitat immediately?

ANSWER > > > >

Rivers are dynamic, active systems. They expand, they erode, they move in new directions, they carry sediment, and they sometimes share more water than their neighbors would like.

• • • • • • • •

Ice ages and human meddling change habitats slowly. However, the Earth speeds things up the old-fashioned way: with volcanoes, floods, earthquakes, and landslides. The faster, the scarier.

QUESTION 164

WHAT do we mean when we describe an organism's physiology?

ANSWER > > > >

• • • • • • • • •

QUESTION 165

WHAT are the three kinds of functions in an organism?

ANSWER > > > >

ANSWER 164

It's the study of the structure and function of the organism.

• • • • • • • • •

ANSWER 165

Mechanical, chemical, and physical functions.

QUESTION 166

WHAT are the three parts of an organ system?

ANSWER > > > >

• • • • • • • • •

QUESTION 167

WHICH part of an organ system can be fatal if it fails?

ANSWER > > > >

ANSWER **166**

Individual organs, tissues, and cells. (If you said keyboard, pipes, and a stool, you'd also be right, but for different reasons.)

• • • • • • • • •

ANSWER **167**

All of them: Failure of the organs, tissues, or cells can be fatal. Or, on a better day, failure could just give you a bad stomachache.

QUESTION 168

WHAT two parts of an animal's structural framework are necessary for movement?

ANSWER >>>>

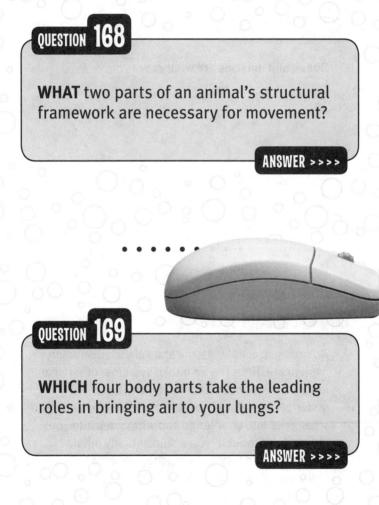

QUESTION 169

WHICH four body parts take the leading roles in bringing air to your lungs?

ANSWER >>>>

ANSWER **168**

Bones and muscles are what move you.

• • • • • • • • •

ANSWER **169**

According to your lungs, the stars of your respiratory
system are, first, the air intake systems, otherwise
known as your nose and mouth. Next, the
underrated epiglottis (part of your voice box) decides
what goes into your lungs and what goes into your
stomach. Without it, you would actually inhale
your food. And finally the trachea, or windpipe,
channels all that fresh air straight to your lungs.

QUESTION 170

WHAT exactly is the main reason you even have a respiratory system?

ANSWER > > > >

• • • • • • • • •

QUESTION 171

WHICH two genders are necessary for sexual reproduction?

ANSWER > > > >

OUTSMART SCIENCE

ANSWER **170**

Your respiratory system (from lips to lungs and beyond) has the endless task of getting oxygen from out there and bringing it into your body. Once you've got it, the oxygen is very quickly distributed via your circulatory system to all of your tissues (which are responsible for making those never-ending requests for oxygen).

• • • • • • • • •

ANSWER **171**

Male and female. The male provides the sperm, and the female provides the egg.

BIOLOGY

QUESTION 172

WHICH parent determines the gender of its animal offspring?

ANSWER > > > >

• • • • • • • • •

QUESTION 173

WHAT is the job of the placenta during pregnancy?

ANSWER > > > >

KAPLAN) **173**

ANSWER 172

The male. He provides either the Y chromosome (male) or the X chromosome (female). The female provides only the X chromosome (female).

• • • • • • • • •

ANSWER 173

To provide nutrition to the fetus and to remove waste.

QUESTION **174**

WHAT are the four parts of a flowering plant's reproductive system?

ANSWER > > > >

• • • • • • • • • •

QUESTION **175**

WHICH part of the human eye changes size depending on the available light?

ANSWER > > > >

Pollen, ovules, seeds, and fruit.

• • • • • • • • •

The pupil. It dilates (opens larger) in low light to let more light in, and it contracts (becomes smaller) in bright light to keep the light from burning little holes into your brain. Kidding.

QUESTION 176

WHAT is the name of the part of the ear that actually does the hearing?

ANSWER > > > >

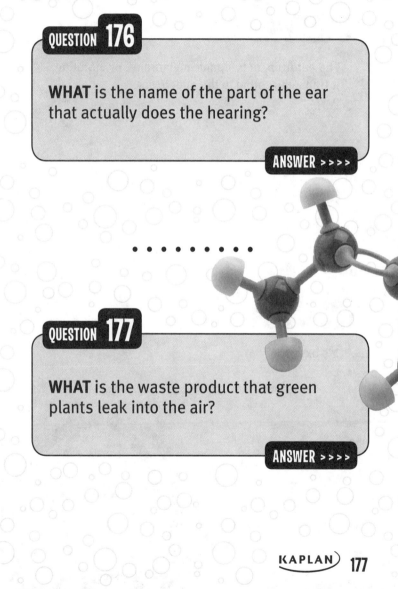

QUESTION 177

WHAT is the waste product that green plants leak into the air?

ANSWER > > > >

The eardrum, or tympanic membrane. By vibrating, it transmits sound to the middle ear.

• • • • • • • • •

It's oxygen.

QUESTION 178

WHAT do plants call their ability to turn sunlight into energy?

ANSWER > > > >

• • • • • • • • •

QUESTION 179

WHAT chemical allows plants to photosynthesize and grow?

ANSWER > > > >

ANSWER 178

If the plants speak English, they call it photosynthesis. In Spanish it's *fotosíntesis*.

• • • • • • • • •

ANSWER 179

Chlorophyll. And it's also responsible for giving them their lovely shades of green.

QUESTION 180

WHAT do we call a plant's little energy-gathering solar panels that make chlorophyll?

ANSWER > > > >

• • • • • • • • • •

QUESTION 181

WHY do leaves change color in the fall?

ANSWER > > > >

ANSWER **180**

We call them chloroplasts.

• • • • • • • • •

ANSWER **181**

Leaves don't change color—those bright autumn colors are the original colors. The green you see in summer comes from chlorophyll, which fades in the cold, dim weather. You could say that leaves change color in the spring, not the fall.

QUESTION 182

WHAT are the three main ingredients of seawater?

ANSWER > > > >

. . . .

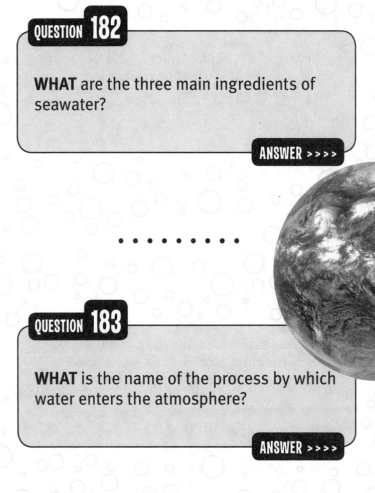

QUESTION 183

WHAT is the name of the process by which water enters the atmosphere?

ANSWER > > > >

ANSWER **182**

They call it H_2O. H is for hydrogen. O is for oxygen. And salt—the extra ingredient in seawater—is for popcorn.

• • • • • • • • •

ANSWER **183**

It's called evaporation. The sun makes the water warmer, warm water becomes steam (or vapor), and up it goes. But don't worry, it'll be back.

QUESTION 184

WHAT is the name of the process by which evaporated water turns back into liquid?

ANSWER > > > >

• • • • • • • •

QUESTION 185

WHAT is the name of the process by which condensed water returns to Earth?

ANSWER > > > >

ANSWER 184

That's condensation. As the air gets colder, the vapor forms clouds. And you know what comes next.

• • • • • • • •

ANSWER 185

When it rains it pours, and when it pours, it's precipitation. Clouds full of condensed vapor are heavy, so ultimately they return water to the rivers, seas, and oceans.

QUESTION **186**

WHAT is the name of the process by which precipitation refills the rivers, seas, and oceans?

ANSWER > > > >

• • • • • • • • •

QUESTION **187**

WHAT are the four most common forms of precipitation?

ANSWER > > > >

ANSWER 186

It's called collection. And once the water is back in place, it's ready to evaporate all over again.

• • • • • • • • •

ANSWER 187

In order of the author's preference: snow, rain, hail, and sleet. The author loves snow, and likes the occasional rainstorm, but can really do without sleet. And hail, under the right circumstances, is pretty cool.

QUESTION 188

WHICH major sources provide our planet's drinking water?

ANSWER > > > >

• • • • • • • • •

QUESTION 189

WHAT on Earth is the atmosphere?

ANSWER > > > >

ANSWER 188

The fresh water we drink comes from wells and other underground sources, as well as from lakes, rivers, glaciers, and plastic bottles.

• • • • • • • •

ANSWER 189

The atmosphere involves everything in the air.

QUESTION 190

WHAT must be present (in addition to your eyes) so you can see something?

ANSWER > > > >

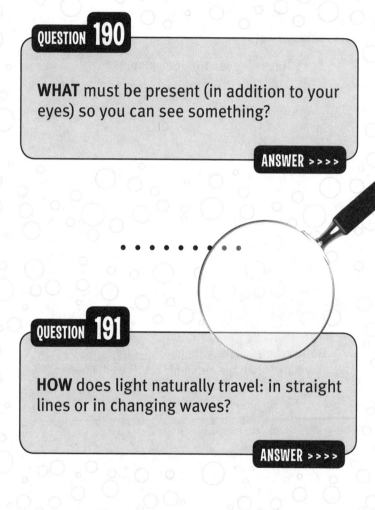

QUESTION 191

HOW does light naturally travel: in straight lines or in changing waves?

ANSWER > > > >

ANSWER 190

Light. This was not a trick question.

• • • • • • • • •

ANSWER 191

Light travels in straight lines, as long as it's traveling through a medium that doesn't change.

BIOLOGY

QUESTION **192**

WHAT is equal to the angle of reflection in a light beam?

ANSWER >>>>

• • • • • • • • •

QUESTION **193**

WHAT is white light?

ANSWER >>>>

ANSWER 192

The angle of incidence. What's that, you ask? First, you have to know the normal. (That's the imaginary line that's always perpendicular to the surface.) When the surface is exactly horizontal, the normal is exactly vertical. If the angle of reflection comes in at a 50 degree angle from the surface, the remaining 40 degrees between the reflection and the right angle of the normal is the angle of incidence.

• • • • • • • •

ANSWER 193

White light is a mixture of many colors, which are each a different wavelength. On the flip side, black is not a color, but the total absence of color.

QUESTION 194

WHERE can you find simple lenses?

ANSWER > > > >

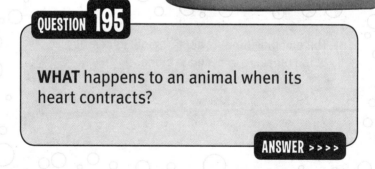

QUESTION 195

WHAT happens to an animal when its heart contracts?

ANSWER > > > >

ANSWER **194**

In telescopes, microscopes, magnifying glasses, camera lenses, and the eye.

• • • • • • • • •

ANSWER **195**

The pumping heart is doing its job, generating blood pressure to circulate blood.

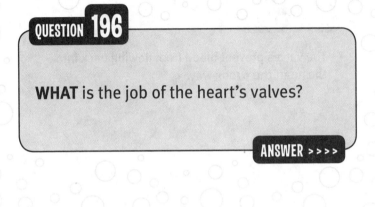

QUESTION **196**

WHAT is the job of the heart's valves?

ANSWER > > > >

• • • • • • • • • •

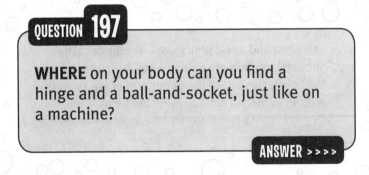

QUESTION **197**

WHERE on your body can you find a hinge and a ball-and-socket, just like on a machine?

ANSWER > > > >

ANSWER **196**

The valves prevent blood from flowing back into the heart the wrong way.

• • • • • • • • •

ANSWER **197**

The wrist and ankle joints work like hinges. The shoulder and hip are ball-and-socket joints, where the ball at the end of the upper arm or leg swivels around in the socket that joins the torso.

QUESTION 198

WHICH common element is so common and so flexible, it has a main role in the chemistry of living organisms?

ANSWER >>>>

. . . .

ANSWER 198

Carbon. It can combine in many ways and is so
very everywhere that finding the age of the carbon
in any organism (carbon dating) is the scientific
means of telling the object's age.

• • • • • • • • •

B
O
N
U
S

Q
U
E
S
T
I
O
N
S

QUESTION 199

WHICH two key factors prompt evolution and diversity of species?

ANSWER >>>>

• • • • • • • • •

QUESTION 200

WHICH elements are found in the molecules of every living organism?

ANSWER >>>>

ANSWER 199

Genetic variation will make the difference and
environmental factors will, too.

• • • • • • • • •

ANSWER 200

Hydrogen, nitrogen, oxygen, carbon, phosphorus,
and sulfur.

QUESTION 201

WHAT do ecologists study?

ANSWER > > > >

• • • • • • • • • •

QUESTION 202

WHAT is an ecosystem?

ANSWER > > > >

ANSWER 201

Ecologists study the many ways that living things interact with their environment—and how environments affect living things. You could also say that ecologists study the ecology, but isn't that obvious?

• • • • • • • • •

ANSWER 202

An ecosystem is an interconnected group of living things. Animals, plants, insects, and more create delicate biotic communities as big as an ocean or as small as a garden.

QUESTION 203

WHAT is the biggest threat to any ecosystem?

ANSWER > > > >

• • • • • • • • •

QUESTION 204

WHAT is an ecological footprint?

ANSWER > > > >

ANSWER 203

Humans are nature's most natural disrupters. Whether we overfish the oceans, overbuild our neighborhoods, or overpollute our air, human carelessness causes imbalance and puts the eeek! into the world's ecosystems.

• • • • • • • •

ANSWER 204

What sounds like a shoe tread is actually a measure of the amount of land, water, and other natural resources needed by the human population of a specific area. The ecological footprint of a city block in Manhattan is far greater than that of a farm in Kansas. Waste products are also measured.

QUESTION **205**

WHAT is sustainability?

ANSWER > > > >

• • • • • • • • •

QUESTION **206**

WHAT is adaptation?

ANSWER > > > >

ANSWER 205

Any ecologist will tell you that the official definition of sustainability is "meeting the needs of the present generation (natural resources, open space, protected species, etc.) without compromising the ability of future generations to meet their own." That ecologist will also tell you that this generation is barely leaving future generations enough to sustain themselves with.

• • • • • • • • •

ANSWER 206

Roughly translated, adaptation means "changing whatever traits need changing in order to help a species live longer." Adaptation improves an organism's odds of survival—and reproduction—in the world.

QUESTION 207

HOW is matter transferred between organisms in a food web?

ANSWER > > > >

• • • • • • • •

QUESTION 208

HOW does energy first enter an ecosphere?

ANSWER > > > >

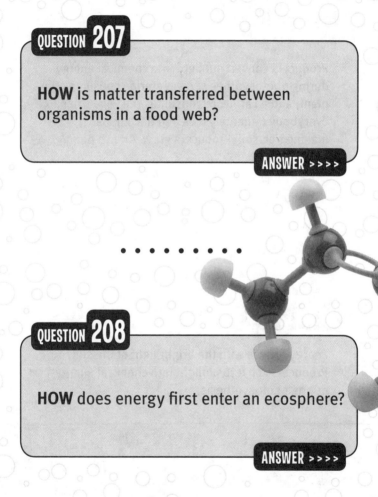

ANSWER 207

Producers convert sunlight into chemical energy during photosynthesis. A vegetarian consumes the plant, and a carnivore consumes the vegetarian. Everybody ultimately dies and decomposes, making rich soil. Producers grow. And so on.

• • • • • • • • •

ANSWER 208

Energy arrives with the bright light of the sun. Producers convert sunlight into chemical energy during photosynthesis.

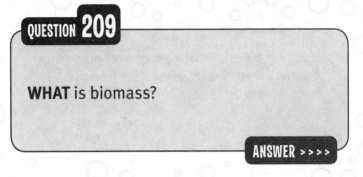

QUESTION **209**

WHAT is biomass?

ANSWER > > > >

• • • • • • • • • •

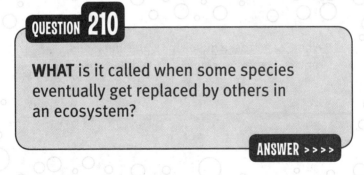

QUESTION **210**

WHAT is it called when some species eventually get replaced by others in an ecosystem?

ANSWER > > > >

OUTSMART SCIENCE

ANSWER 209

If you combine the total mass of every organism in a particular ecosystem, you get the biomass. (Bio + mass = get it?)

• • • • • • • • •

ANSWER 210

When a species, a queen, or a president gets replaced by something else, it's called succession.

QUESTION 211

WHAT are some of the many tools used by scientists to collect data?

ANSWER > > > >

QUESTION 212

WHAT is the difference between a topographic map and a geologic map?

ANSWER > > > >

ANSWER 211

Pen, pencil, paper, chalkboard, computer, calculator, microscope, magnifying glass, binoculars, telescope, camera, scale, stethoscope, and on and on.

• • • • • • • • •

ANSWER 212

A topographic map shows the natural and man-made features of a place, including landscape and elevations. A geologic map shows the geology of an area: the sedimentary, igneous and volcanic formations, and geologic structures (like folds and faults). Neither is a political map, which tells you what city or country you're in and, like politics, is always subject to change.

QUESTION **213**

WHAT is a scale map?

ANSWER > > > >

· · · · · · · · · ·

QUESTION **214**

WHAT is a hypothesis?

ANSWER > > > >

ANSWER 213

A scale map shows a printed area that's a percentage of the actual area it represents. If a 10-inch map reflects a ten-mile area, the scale is one inch equals one mile. If it's a map of the solar system, one inch could be 100 million miles.

• • • • • • • • •

ANSWER 214

A hypothesis is a theory about the natural world that tries to explain certain facts or observations.

QUESTION 215

WHICH of Earth's energy sources are nonrenewable?

ANSWER > > > >

• • • • • • • • •

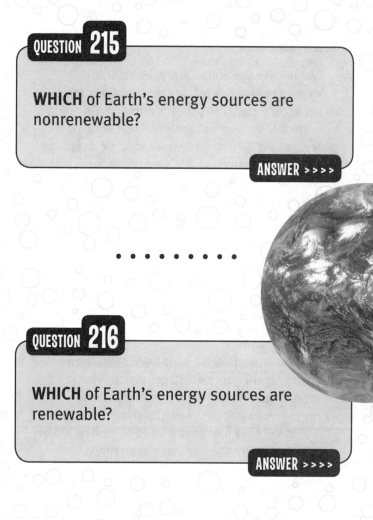

QUESTION 216

WHICH of Earth's energy sources are renewable?

ANSWER > > > >

ANSWER 215

Like the most popular library books, some sources of energy can't be renewed. Coal, for instance. Once you use it, it's burnt up. Gone. Up in smoke. Nothing left behind. Same goes for oil and gas. And if you really want to name an energy source you'd never want to renew, that's nuclear energy. Its endless barrels of toxic byproduct are a total waste.

. . . .

ANSWER 216

The Sun (solar panels), wind (windmills), water (hydroelectric generators), geysers and hot springs (geothermal exchange pumps), and certain crops (biofuel converters) are renewable. It is actually easy being green, and some day, it'll be easier to power your life more naturally.

QUESTION 217

WHAT is plastic made from?

ANSWER >>>>

• • • • • • • • •

QUESTION 218

WHICH of the numbers—from 1 to 7—stamped on a plastic container represent plastic that's recyclable?

ANSWER >>>>

ANSWER 217

Everything plastic, including a higher percentage of your clothing than you'd care to know, is made from petrochemicals. The chemicals part is no surprise. The petro part is oil. That's right. You're wearing oil. As oil prices go up (and supplies go down), so too will the prices you pay for your cola bottle, your garden hose, your computer keyboard, your eyeglass frames, and those stylish former plastic bottles that are now your fleece jacket. Paper or plastic?

• • • • • • • • •

ANSWER 218

It's as easy as 1 and 2. Type 1 is mainly for water and soda bottles. Type 2 is for milk bottles, detergent bottles, and many plastic bags. Some Type 4 plastic (garment bags and shrink wrap) can be recycled. Rarely can the rest. But the worst offender is Type 7, mixed or layered plastic, which has no redeeming (or redeemable) features and must be landfilled.

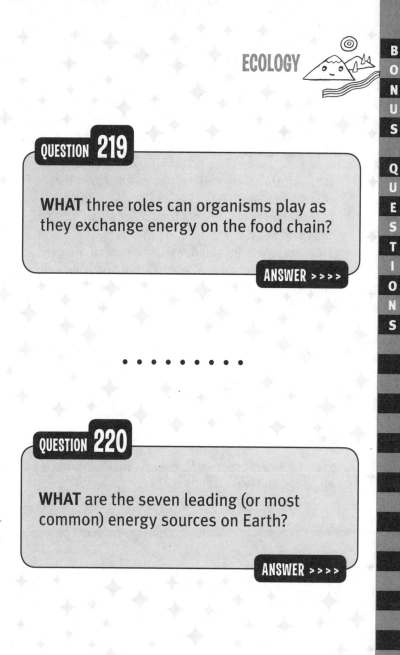

QUESTION **219**

WHAT three roles can organisms play as they exchange energy on the food chain?

ANSWER > > > >

• • • • • • • • •

QUESTION **220**

WHAT are the seven leading (or most common) energy sources on Earth?

ANSWER > > > >

ANSWER 219

1. Producers are organisms, like green plants, that others find tasty.
2. Consumers get nutrients from other organisms and find them tasty.
3. Decomposers (or saprobes) convert dead things into substances that are definitely not tasty, but help producers grow.

· · · · · · · · ·

ANSWER 220

In alphabetical order: coal, gas, hydroelectric, nuclear, oil, solar, and wind.

QUESTION 221

WHICH word best describes the state of everything on Earth, in the solar system, and in the universe: stasis or flux?

ANSWER > > > >

QUESTION 222

WHICH of the eight original planets in our solar system are gas planets?

ANSWER > > > >

ANSWER 221

Flux! In a state of flux, everything is constantly changing—whether it's growing, decaying, moving, or otherwise evolving. With stasis, nothing changes.

• • • • • • • •

ANSWER 222

Five, six, seven, and eight: Jupiter, Saturn, Uranus, and Neptune are each composed mainly of gases. In fact, if Saturn could be lowered into water, it would actually float. These four "gas giants" make up 99 percent of the mass orbiting our Sun.

QUESTION 223

WHICH planets in our solar system are terrestrial, and what in the world does that mean?

ANSWER > > > >

• • • • • • • • • •

QUESTION 224

WHAT is Pluto made of?

ANSWER > > > >

ANSWER 223

One, two, three, and four: Mercury, Venus, Mars, and especially Earth are made of earth. (That's what terrestrial means, you Earthling.)

• • • • • • • • •

ANSWER 224

The former planet (not the dog) is mostly ice, with some rock mixed in. It's two-thirds the size of Earth's moon and 4.3 billion miles away. You'd hate it there. You'd only get a birthday once every 249 years.

QUESTION 225

HOW many years old is our solar system: 1.6 billion, 4.6 billion, or 9.6 billion years?

ANSWER > > > >

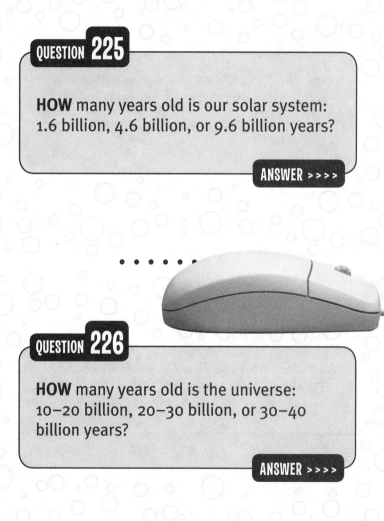

QUESTION 226

HOW many years old is the universe: 10–20 billion, 20–30 billion, or 30–40 billion years?

ANSWER > > > >

Our solar system is 4.6 billion years old. Compared with the universe, that's still kind of young.

• • • • • • • • •

The universe is only 10–20 billion years old. And you thought your parents were old.

QUESTION 227

WHAT is the closest astronomical object to the planet Earth?

ANSWER >>>>

• • • • • • • • • •

QUESTION 228

WHAT is the Sun made of?

ANSWER >>>>

ANSWER 227

If you don't count man-made satellites, failing space stations, and random asteroids, the answer is the Moon.

• • • • • • • • •

ANSWER 228

The Sun is a ball of burning gas. Most of it (70 percent) is hydrogen, and 28 percent is helium.

QUESTION 229

HOW does the Sun rank in size compared to other stars: above average, below average, or average?

ANSWER > > > >

• • • • • • • • •

QUESTION 230

HOW many Earths would fit inside the Sun if it were hollow?

ANSWER > > > >

Average. The Sun is about 865,000 miles in diameter. Other stars are as much as 1,500 times larger.

• • • • • • • • •

About 1.3 million Earths would fit inside. Imagine filling a basketball (Sun) with sesame seeds (Earths).

QUESTION 231

WHY is there a "dark side of the Moon"?

ANSWER >>>>

• • • • • • • • •

QUESTION 232

WHY can't we see a new moon?

ANSWER >>>>

ANSWER 231

Because the Moon doesn't revolve as it orbits Earth. The so-called "light side" always faces us, and the so-called "dark side" is always turned away. Actually, neither side is always light or dark: Each has days just like we do.

• • • • • • • • •

ANSWER 232

The new moon occurs when the Earth, the Sun, and the Moon are in a straight line. The Earth is in the middle, and it's casting a shadow on the Moon.

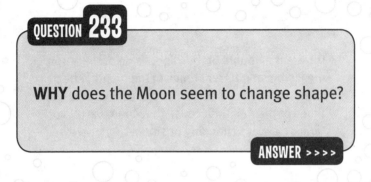

QUESTION **233**

WHY does the Moon seem to change shape?

ANSWER > > > >

• • • • • • • • •

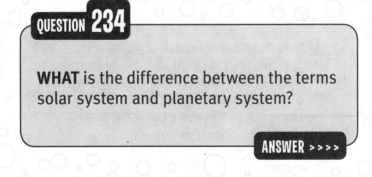

QUESTION **234**

WHAT is the difference between the terms solar system and planetary system?

ANSWER > > > >

ANSWER 233

Different amounts of the "light" side of the Moon
are visible at different times of the month. The
Moon seems like a circle or a crescent at different
times of the month because the Moon, Earth, and
Sun are always changing positions.

• • • • • • • • •

ANSWER 234

A planetary system is any group of planets
(and their moons) orbiting a star, or stars—plus
whatever asteroids, meteoroids, and comets
are caught in the stellar gravity. But there's only
one solar system, and that's ours—the planetary
system that orbits the sun named Sol.

QUESTION 235

WHY does the Earth revolve around the Sun?

ANSWER > > > >

• • • • • • • • •

QUESTION 236

WHAT is a galaxy?

ANSWER > > > >

ANSWER 235

Because the Earth is caught in the Sun's gravitational attraction. It's an attraction that has lasted for more than four billion years.

• • • • • • • • •

ANSWER 236

A galaxy is a massive star cluster. Some have a few million stars, others have over a trillion stars clinging together. All these stars share a common center of gravity. Our galaxy is called the Milky Way, and there are billions more next door.

QUESTION **237**

HOW many stars are in the Milky Way galaxy: about 100, about 100 thousand, about 100 million, or about 100 billion?

ANSWER >>>>

· · · · · · · · ·

QUESTION **238**

WHAT does a light-year measure?

ANSWER >>>>

ANSWER 237

There are about 100 billion stars in our galaxy.
And it's not nearly the biggest one.

• • • • • • • • •

ANSWER 238

A light-year measures distance, not time. It's used
to measure gigantic distances. It's the amount
of distance that light travels in a year: six trillion
(6,000,000,000,000) miles.

QUESTION 239

HOW wide is the Milky Way, in light years?

ANSWER > > > >

. . . .

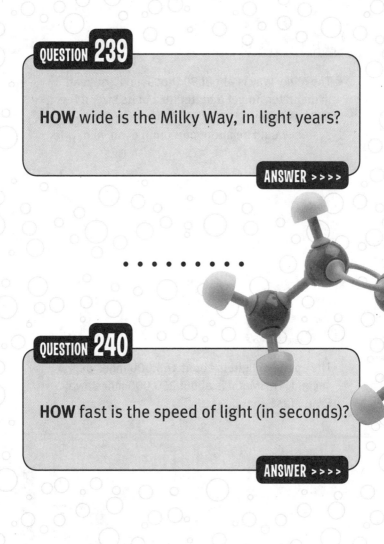

QUESTION 240

HOW fast is the speed of light (in seconds)?

ANSWER > > > >

OUTSMART SCIENCE

ANSWER 239

The Milky Way is about 90 thousand light-years in diameter. To get a better idea of its size: If the Milky Way were 100 miles in diameter, our solar system would be about one-tenth of an inch wide.

• • • • • • • • •

ANSWER 240

The speed of light is about 186,000 miles per second. The Moon is about 250,000 miles away. Pretty fast.

QUESTION **241**

HOW far is the Sun from the Earth?

ANSWER > > > >

• • • • • • • • • •

QUESTION **242**

HOW old is sunlight by the time it reaches Earth?

ANSWER > > > >

ANSWER 241

About 93 million miles, more or less.

• • • • • • • • •

ANSWER 242

It takes just over eight minutes for sunlight to travel 93 million miles. So, if the Sun suddenly stops working, we'll have about 480 extra seconds to work on our tans.

ASTRONOMY

QUESTION 243

HOW far is Venus from Earth?

ANSWER >>>>

• • • • • • • • • •

QUESTION 244

HOW far is Earth from Mars?

ANSWER >>>>

ANSWER **243**

About 28 million miles away. Venus and Earth are always moving, like sumo wrestlers, so it's hard to be exact.

ANSWER **244**

Earth is about 50 million miles from Mars. Using current rocket technology, it would take about four months to get there. Using a car, it would take even longer.

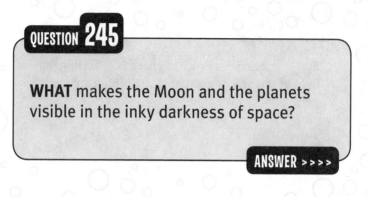

QUESTION 245

WHAT makes the Moon and the planets visible in the inky darkness of space?

ANSWER >>>>

• • • • • • • • •

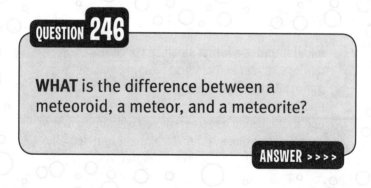

QUESTION 246

WHAT is the difference between a meteoroid, a meteor, and a meteorite?

ANSWER >>>>

ANSWER 245

Every rock and near-rock in space is reflecting the light of the Sun or another star. Nothing but a star generates its own light.

• • • • • • • •

ANSWER 246

A meteoroid is a rather small space chunk (under 170 feet in diameter) entering a planet's atmosphere. Whether it's mineral or ice, as it heats up during entry it gets a bright tail of glowing gas, and that's called a meteor. (If you wish upon it, it's called a shooting star.) Any fragment that actually reaches the ground is called a meteorite.

QUESTION 247

WHAT are the eight planets, from largest to smallest?

ANSWER >>>>

• • • • • • • • •

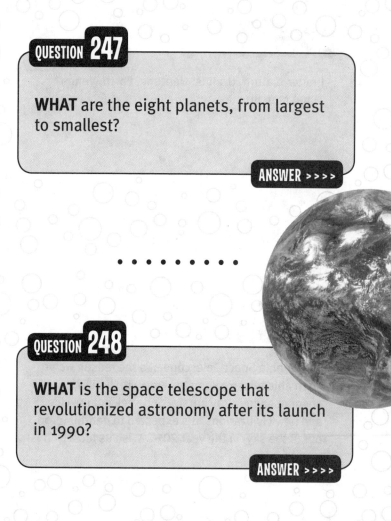

QUESTION 248

WHAT is the space telescope that revolutionized astronomy after its launch in 1990?

ANSWER >>>>

ANSWER 247

Jupiter, Saturn, Uranus, Neptune, Earth, Venus, Mars, Mercury.

• • • • • • • • •

ANSWER 248

The Hubble Space Telescope. It's the reason we've been able to see a comet collide with Jupiter, observe gamma-ray bursts, and seek out new life and new civilizations. It's expected to deorbit (drop out of the sky) in the year 2010. Wish us luck!

WHICH two planets have the asteroid belt between them?

ANSWER > > > >

• • • • • • • • • •

QUESTION 250

HOW long is a year on Mercury?
On Jupiter?

ANSWER > > > >

OUTSMART SCIENCE

ANSWER 249

Between Mars and Jupiter, there is a group of up to a million objects, smaller than planets, usually smaller than a mile across, and sometimes smaller than pebbles. The gravity of Jupiter and the Sun helps hold them in orbit. They are dangerous to spaceships and are good protection against an attack from Saturn.

· · · · · · · · ·

ANSWER 250

Every planet goes around the Sun in a different orbit, so their years are of different lengths. On Mercury, a year is 88 days long. On Jupiter, your birthday comes every 11.86 Earth years.